A REASON FOR

HOPE

IN A TIME OF TRAGEDY

CROSSWAY BOOKS

A DIVISION OF
GOOD NEWS PUBLISHERS
WHEATON, ILLINOIS

A Reason for Hope

Copyright © 2001 by Good News Publishers

Published by Crossway Books

        A division of Good News Publishers

        1300 Crescent Street

        Wheaton, Illinois 60187

Cover design: Cindy Kiple

Cover photo: Corbis Sigma

First printing, 2001

Printed in the United States of America

ISBN 1-58134-395-7

References marked NIV are taken from *Holy Bible: New International Version*®, copyright © 1973, 1978, 1984 by International Bible Society. Used by permission of Zondervan Publishing House. All rights reserved.

The "NIV" and "New International Version" trademarks are registered in the United States Patent and Trademark Office by International Bible Society. Use of either trademark requires the permission of International Bible Society.

References marked KJV are from the King James Version.

References marked RSV are from *Revised Standard Version,* copyright © 1946, 1971 by Division of Education of the National Council of Churches of Christ in the United States of America.

References marked NASB are from the *New American Standard Bible,* copyright © 1960, 1962, 1963, 1968, 1971, 1972, 1973, 1975, 1977, 1988, and 1995 by The Lockman Foundation and are used by permission.

References marked ESV are from *The Holy Bible, English Standard Version,* copyright © 2001 by Crossway Bibles, a division of Good News Publishers.

Good News Publishers (including Crossway Books) is a not-for-profit organization that exists solely for the purpose of publishing the good news of the Gospel and the truth of God's Word, the Bible.

15	14	13	12	11	10	09	08	07	06	05	04	03	02	01
15	14	13	12	11	10	9	8	7	6	5	4	3	2	1

CONTENTS

PUBLISHER'S PREFACE

Lane T. Dennis

September 11, 2001 is a day that we will never forget. In the wake of the unthinkable tragedy and evil of that day, we have been changed forever. Suddenly what seemed so solid, so permanent, so enduring has become fleeting and precarious. How fragile life is. How quickly we can be swept into eternity. In response to the overwhelming loss of life and loved ones, we have been moved to tears and sorrow at the deepest level.

But September 11 also saw the beginning of something unexpected and extraordinary—a day when we saw the outpouring of compassion, acts of heroism, and a turning back to God for refuge and strength.

This book then is a book of hope. It is a book that contains the unforgettable testimony of Lisa Beamer—as she writes in the foreword of her husband, Todd Beamer, who gave his life to subdue the terrorists on Flight #93, and as she tells of her unshakable faith in God and his sustaining grace in the midst of overwhelming personal loss.

It is a book that includes nine resounding messages of hope

and prayer, messages given by Christian leaders in the days and hours immediately following September 11.

This is a book too that includes words of commendation and assurance from the President of our country, reminding us, as he wrote in a letter for Todd Beamer's memorial service at Wheaton College, that "nothing, not even death, can separate us from God's love."

What is the reason for the hope we have, this hope that cannot be shaken even by these events? On the morning of September 11, before the events of the day began to unfold, my Bible reading included Psalm 11 and the words "if the foundations are destroyed, what can the righteous do?" (verse 3, ESV). What is the answer? We saw our foundations being destroyed, but we also saw a great outpouring of compassion and heroic action in response.

But at the most basic level, the answer is to return to God and to his eternal Word. As the prophet Isaiah wrote, "The grass withers, the flower fades, but the word of our God will stand forever" (Isaiah 40:8, ESV). The answer is to be found in the written Word of God, the Bible. More than this, the answer is to be found in the living Word of God—in Jesus Christ, God's only Son, who bears our sins and griefs and sorrows; who gives us a living hope through faith in his atoning death and resurrection.

Though our foundations may have been shaken, they have not been destroyed. For our hope is in the living God and in his eternal Word. That is the reason for our hope—the reason that is retold so clearly and powerfully in the pages of this book. To God alone be the glory.

Lane T. Dennis, Ph.D.
President and Publisher
Crossway Books

Note: Author royalties and publishing net income from the sale of *A Reason for Hope* are being donated to **The Todd Beamer Foundation**, P.O. Box 32, Cranbury, NJ 08512. The mission of the Foundation includes meeting the long-term needs of children who lost a parent in the events of September 11th, assisting future victims of terrorism, and continuing Todd's passion for mentoring and equipping youth to make the same heroic choices he did throughout his life. For additional information, visit the Foundation website, www.beamerfoundation.org.

FOREWORD

Lisa Beamer

The mention of September 11 brings to mind floods of memories and emotions for all of us. For most Americans, feelings of sadness, disbelief, anger and frustration prevail. Added to these for my family is the incredible personal pain of the loss of Todd, our husband, father, son and brother. With only these human emotions to draw upon I'm afraid I wouldn't be able to even breathe at times. The good news (yes, there is good news!) is that God is faithful each moment to provide the supernatural resources I need not only to carry on, but to be even joyful on occasion. He is showing me his eternal perspective in ways I could not have imagined before September 11. He is giving me peace and steadiness at a time when these are humanly unexplainable. He is showering me with help from the people of his church before I ask or even know what it is I need. Yes, this grieving is hard and will be a long road, but it is never without hope that God is sovereign and loving in our world and in my life.

Truly we have lost much, but we have gained much as well. As Joseph said to his brothers in Genesis 50:20 I say now to the originators of the evil acts of September 11, "You intended to harm me, but God intended it for good to accomplish what is now being done, the saving of many lives." God enabled Todd and his fellow passengers on Flight 93 to take uncommon and courageous actions that undoubtedly saved many lives here on earth. God is now enabling us as survivors to be equally courageous in saving many lives for eternity as we spread the word of his love and his plan of eternal salvation to lost and searching souls. Although I suffer indescribable human pain, the knowledge of God's eternal good coming from these events is an unwavering anchor for me and will be for our boys someday as well.

Last week I was sorting through some papers in Todd's office and came across this quote, which he had kept at the bottom of his in-box for the past few years. I don't know his thoughts in keeping this in circulation, but it certainly seems prophetic in light of the turn his life took on September 11. It is a quote by Theodore Roosevelt: "The credit belongs to the man who is actually in the arena, who strives valiantly; who knows the great enthusiasms, the great devotions, and spends himself in a worthy cause; who, at best, knows the triumph of high achievement; and who, at worst, if he fails, at least fails while daring greatly, so that his place shall never be with those cold and timid souls who know neither victory nor defeat."

On September 11, Todd's mission on earth was completed, and he ended daring greatly—not with the cold and timid souls who know neither victory nor defeat. Our challenge in the time remaining for us is to each day dare greatly for God, leaving lukewarm faith behind.

I covet your prayers now and in the future as the boys and I face the challenges of life each day without Todd. I thank you in advance for the blessings these will bring for us.

I pray, too, as you face the challenges of each day that you will know that you are never without hope, through faith that is founded in the sovereign, loving God. As you read the words of this book, may you be strengthened in hope and courage, to dare greatly for God, leaving lukewarm faith behind.

Lisa Beamer

LETTER FROM THE PRESIDENT

George W. Bush

The following letter from President George W. Bush was read at the memorial service for Todd Beamer by the Honorable J. Dennis Hastert, Speaker of the House of Representatives, on the 6th of October, 2001, at Wheaton College, Wheaton, Illinois. Todd and Lisa (Brosious) Beamer, both members of the Wheaton College Class of 1991, had planned to attend their tenth anniversary class reunion. Speaker Hastert is a member of the Wheaton College class of 1964.

THE WHITE HOUSE

WASHINGTON

October 5, 2001

As you gather -- members of a class and a community -- our Nation stands with you in grief and gratitude. We feel grief for the loss of a husband, father, and friend -- a man who was deeply loved by his family, his friends, and by God. We feel gratitude for Todd Beamer's example of courage and his wife Lisa's example of grace.

On September 11, Americans saw terrible evil. We also saw how a man can face evil: soberly, directly, without flinching. Our entire Nation now knows what bravery looks like. And we will not forget.

Wheaton College stands for things that endure: for faith and integrity, and for service to others. Those very values found expression in the life and sacrifice of Todd Beamer. Today, we thank God for a good man. We pray for his family and friends in a time of sorrow. And we affirm the faith in which Todd shared, knowing that nothing, not even death, can separate us from God's love.

America Prays:
"Do It Again, Lord"

Max Lucado

Dear Lord,

We're still hoping we'll wake up. We're still hoping we'll open a sleepy eye and think, *What a horrible dream.*

But we won't, will we, Father? What we saw was not a dream. Planes did gouge towers. Flames did consume our fortress. People did perish. It was no dream and, dear Father, we are sad.

There is a ballet dancer who will no longer dance and a doctor who will no longer heal. A church has lost her priest, a classroom is minus a teacher. Cora ran a food pantry. Paige was a counselor and Dana, dearest Father, Dana was only three years old. (Who held her in those final moments?)

We are sad, Father. For as the innocent are buried, our innocence is buried as well. We thought we were safe. Perhaps we should have known better. But we didn't.

And so we come to you. We don't ask you for help; we beg you for it. We don't request it; we implore it. We know what you can do. We've read the accounts. We've pondered the stories and now we plead, Do it again, Lord. Do it again.

Remember Joseph? You rescued him from the pit. You can do the same for us. Do it again, Lord.

Remember the Hebrews in Egypt? You protected their children from the angel of death. We have children, too, Lord. Do it again.

And Sarah? Remember her prayers? You heard them. Joshua? Remember his fears? You inspired him. The women at the tomb? You resurrected their hope. The doubts of Thomas? You took them away. Do it again, Lord. Do it again.

You changed Daniel from a captive into a king's counselor. You took Peter the fisherman and made him Peter an apostle. Because of you, David went from leading sheep to leading armies. Do it again, Lord, for we need counselors today, Lord. We need apostles. We need leaders. Do it again, dear Lord.

Most of all, do again what you did at Calvary. What we saw here on that Tuesday, you saw there on that Friday. Innocence slaughtered. Goodness murdered. Mothers weeping. Evil dancing. Just as the ash fell on our children, the darkness fell on your Son. Just as our towers were shattered, the very Tower of Eternity was pierced.

And by dusk, heaven's sweetest song was silent, buried behind a rock.

But you did not waver, O Lord. You did not waver. After three days in a dark hole, you rolled the rock and rumbled the earth and turned the darkest Friday into the brightest Sunday. Do it again, Lord. Grant us a September Easter.

We thank you, dear Father, for these hours of unity. Disaster has done what discussion could not. Doctrinal fences have fallen. Republicans are standing with Democrats. Skin colors have been covered by the ash of burning buildings. We thank you for these hours of unity.

And we thank you for these hours of prayer. The Enemy sought to bring us to our knees and succeeded. He had no idea, however, that we would kneel before you. And he has no idea what you can do.

Let your mercy be upon our President, Vice President, and their families. Grant to those who lead us wisdom beyond their years and experience. Have mercy upon the souls who have departed and the wounded who remain. Give us grace that we might forgive and faith that we might believe.

And look kindly upon your church. For two thousand years you've used her to heal a hurting world.

Do it again, Lord. Do it again.

Through Christ, Amen.

Written by Max Lucado for "America Prays," a national prayer vigil on September 15, 2001.

GOD IS OUR REFUGE AND STRENGTH

R. Kent Hughes

God is our refuge and strength,
a very present help in trouble.
Therefore we will not fear though the earth gives way,
though the mountains be moved into the heart of the sea,
though its waters roar and foam,
though the mountains tremble at its swelling. . . .
The LORD of hosts is with us;
the God of Jacob is our fortress.

PSALM 46:1-3, 7, ESV

Though we all wish the recent tragedy had not happened, the terrifying images of September 11 (year one of the new millennium) are an unerasable part of our national soul. Try as we may, we will never forget it—even to the point of always knowing where we were when we heard the news. The twin towers of the World Trade Center awash in the bright morning sun—a beautiful day in Manhattan—except that the north tower was billowing black smoke because at 8:45 A.M. American Airlines Flight #11 had disappeared into its side.

How had this happened? we wondered. In a horrific instant we knew, when another jumbo jet (United Airlines Flight #175) came streaming across New York's skyline and banked sharply into the south tower. Death billowed forth, bright orange, 1000 degrees centigrade in the blue sky. And we began to weep.

Twenty minutes later we learned that American Airlines Flight #77 had detonated into the Pentagon. And an hour later United Airlines reported that hijacked Flight #93 had gone down in Shanksville, Pennsylvania. The agony had just begun as we watched the towers become colossal torches billowing black smoke to heaven.

Most of us never dreamed the World Trade towers would

implode. But we all watched in disbelief when in real-life slow motion the south tower roared down through its 110 floors with its great white antenna twisting down like a straw in the vortex—only to be followed by the north tower as it too descended deep into the heart of Manhattan. The vision of people running down Church Street as the cloud of concussion surged after them like a tidal wave is apocalyptic—like the tide of a nuclear winter.

It was all done with "Satanic cunning," as New York pastor Tim Keller described it—first the north tower, and then, with the whole world watching, the south tower. Hellish theater for dark hearts. The suffering is untold. Our hearts break with a mere glance at the TV.

What are we to make of September 11? Foremost, the unbearable theater of that day is a cinematic clip of the depths of the human heart.

> The devil yawned
> And we gazed
> into
> The abyss.

There are simply no limits to human depravity. We should never be surprised as to how far into evil men and women will go—"Their feet are swift to shed blood; in their paths are ruin and misery, and the way of peace they have not known" (Romans 3:15-18, ESV here and in subsequent Scriptures).

But we must not make this observation with smug detachment, because *we are Sept. 11*—if we are left to ourselves apart from God. Clearly, the world is not getting better. It is more dangerous than ever before. That Tuesday's excruciating cinema ought to seal forever the mouths of those who rest their hopes on the evolution of culture. It is a fiction. We have done our best, and we cannot save ourselves. Supernatural deliverance is our only hope. What this world needs is a Savior.

Along with our need, we saw that life is fragile. The World Trade towers epitomized financial affluence and power and security. Each weekday afternoon about 2:30, chauffeured limos lined up for three blocks to pick up busy executives and drive them to their homes on the Hudson and in Connecticut. This was life at the top. But in a second all 700 employees of Cantor Fitzgerald were gone. All thirty floors of Morgan Stanley are no more. God, *"You return man to dust and say, 'Return, O children of man!'" (Psalm 90:3).* Human life is tenuous for all.

Some may view this as judgment on the sinful Big Apple. But we must disabuse ourselves of any such thought. Jesus spoke to his contemporaries (and to us) when he referred to a recent tragedy with the question, "Or those eighteen on whom the tower fell in Siloam and killed them: do you think they were worse offenders than all the others who lived in Jerusalem? No, I tell you; but unless you repent, you will all likewise perish" (Luke 13:4, 5). The falling of the tower of Siloam in Jerusalem was a wake-up call for God's covenant people—just as the fall of the twin towers is to us. God's judgment may be slow (as some count time), but it is sure for all.

These searing revelations are hard to look at. But those who take what happened September 11 to heart—who truly face the depth of human sin, who truly contemplate their own mortality, who understand that judgment is coming to all—will find themselves in the way of grace because it will become ever clearer to them that nothing can meet their needs save a Savior. There is no hope for this world apart from a Savior.

Most notably, we must understand that God is sovereign. The Scriptures are clear that God's power (analogous to creation power) is used to direct the history of mankind. As God himself says, "I form light and create darkness, I make well-being and create calamity, I am the LORD, who does all these things" (Isaiah 45:7). And so in that Tuesday's infamy we see parallel examples of disaster and prosperity.

Barbara Olson, the Solicitor General's wife, changed her flight from Monday to Tuesday so she could be with her husband on his birthday. Her new flight was American Airlines Flight #77, which ended in the Pentagon holocaust.

Jack Zimmermann, previously a member of the congregation I pastor, recently was promoted to a chief executive position with Morgan Stanley in New York, and he moved his family from Chicago to Connecticut. His schedule still required two days a week in Morgan Stanley's Chicago-area office. Jack was in Chicago when United Airlines Flight #175 passed directly through his New York office in the south tower. But I must say that if Jack Zimmermann had perished in New York, it would have been under God's directive sovereignty, for God has lovingly decreed when Jack's life will end "from all eternity . . . in such a year, on such a day, at such an hour, in such a place, in such a manner" (Pascal). The Bible says that God is sovereign in space and time, but it does not pretend that he creates immunity from physical tragedy—at least, not until the end of time.

Why does God permit tragedy? On one level, Christians no more have the answer than anyone else. We have no direct access to the purposes of God in specific events. But as Christians, we do know that God's purposes will in the end be for good. As Australian archbishop Peter Jensen called his hearers to remember, in the memorial service held the next day in Sydney's St. Andrews Cathedral:

> God is in charge, but his Son was crucified. If those two things are true, then somehow we can still believe that goodness will triumph, that God will be exalted, that righteousness will be vindicated. A world in which the Son of God was both crucified and resurrected is a world in which it is possible to have hope in the midst of thickest gloom and sorrow.

The Archbishop went on to point out that:

> Our culture has made it a habit of setting aside the wisdom of the past, especially the Bible. But in the midst of catastrophe, when we are confronted with great realities, the Bible's words suddenly come through with immense power and wisdom. There simply is no other place to turn to bind up the brokenhearted and comfort the bereaved and give wisdom to the simple.*

That Tuesday morning, when I changed my text from Genesis to Psalm 46, I had no idea that the chaplain of the United States Senate would preach it, that Sydney's archbishop and the chaplain at Wheaton College would do the same—and that my preacher-son William Carey Hughes would select it. Neither did I know that Martin Luther had based his hymn "A Mighty Fortress Is Our God" on the opening line of that Psalm. It is apparent to me that Psalm 46 is the Spirit-inspired, Spirit-directed text for his people in America and around the world at this time.

This famous Psalm was written in response to an unidentified crisis in Israel's history. The great city was under attack, evidently surrounded by her enemies. So from the ramparts of Jerusalem its indomitable words sounded in the hearts of her people. In subsequent years, it is believed, it was sung by the temple choirs as an antiphon. What is apparent is that its lyrics soar above the occasion, providing an inspired song to the assaulted.

CONFIDENCE AMIDST A DISINTEGRATING WORLD

The sight of the devastating hordes, surrounding ancient Jerusalem and threatening complete annihilation, led the Psalmist to describe his people's plight in apocalyptic terms that point to the ultimate undoing of all things—a day yet future to us—yet a day with which we, having seen the man-made mountains of Manhattan fall, will find eerie resonance.

God is our refuge and strength,
a very present help in trouble.

Therefore we will not fear though the earth gives way,
though the mountains be moved into the heart of the sea,
though its waters roar and foam,
though the mountains tremble at its swelling.

—vv. 1-3

The Psalm's staggering declaration is this: If the whole world implodes, so that towering mountains (not puny skyscrapers!) fall into the sea—though the world as we know it comes to a roaring convulsive end—*we will not fear.* And why do we have no fear? The answer was thrust forth first in the opening line: "God is our refuge and strength, a very present help in trouble" (v. 1). The emphasis is on the word "God." He, nothing else, is our refuge and strength. Our security is in God alone, not in God *plus* anything else.

When the World Trade Center's towers *descended,* the souls of those who sought refuge in God *ascended* beyond the blue of that September day. If you don't have God, you have nothing. If you have him, you have everything. If your security rests merely on your portfolio, your home, even your lovely family—you will have zero when your end comes.

The theme of the Psalm is right there in verse 1, because when you have God you have a "refuge" (a place to run), and you have "strength" (God within to empower you), and you have an ever-present "help in trouble." This great sustaining theme is repeated twice again in the immortal words of verses 7, 11:

The Lord of hosts is with us;
the God of Jacob is our fortress.

COMFORT FROM GOD'S PRESENCE

In the Psalmist's day Jerusalem was the city of God. In it, God dwelt in the Holy of Holies. But there was no stream in Jerusalem, much less a river. So when the Psalm here describes the city as having a river, it looks beyond Jerusalem to a deeper reality:

> There is a river whose streams make glad the city of God,
>   the holy habitation of the Most High.
> God is in the midst of her; she shall not be moved;
> God will help her when morning dawns.
>
> —vv. 4, 5

In contrast to roaring, foaming waters of destruction, a life-giving river flows through the city of God. Like the river that flowed from Eden to water the world, so this river of God's presence gives life and peace. And its ultimate expression will come in the eternal state—"the river of the water of life, bright as crystal, flowing from the throne of God and of the Lamb through the middle of the street of the city" (Revelation 22:1, 2a). In the words of the beloved hymn, "Like a river glorious is God's perfect peace."

The presence of God with his people makes wherever they are a city of refuge. Those who are in the city of God do not fall—though the world's tallest buildings may fall on them—because the city of God is not confined to a mere locality on earth. We must understand that "morning has broken" for our fallen brothers and sisters in New York and the Pentagon—and they are by the river of God. Such is our confidence.

Furthermore, we will not fear—because, as the Psalmist proclaims,

> The LORD of hosts is with us;
> the God of Jacob is our fortress.
>
> —vv. 7, 11

The "hosts" (the armies of heaven) are under the direction of our ever-present Lord. Recall the orange fireball billowing from the south tower. And then remember how the Lord opened the eyes of Elisha's servant so that "he saw, and behold, the mountain was full of horses and chariots of fire all around Elisha" (2 Kings 6:17)—the armies of heaven clad in fiery orange. The infernal fire of man is nothing before God's chariots of fire. The God of Jacob is a fortress indeed—an unshakable refuge in these uncertain days.

CONFIDENCE AMIDST WAR

The final stanza of Psalm 46 opens with a vision of things to come. We know this because the word for "behold" is used for seeing with an inward eye, as a seer or a prophet sees:

> Come, behold the works of the LORD,
> how he has brought desolations on the earth.
> He makes wars cease to the ends of the earth;
> he breaks the bow and shatters the spear,
> he burns the chariots with fire.
>
> —vv. 8, 9

The world will be forcibly disarmed by God himself. The implements of war will be gathered into great broken mountains on the earth's battlefields—every H-bomb, every missile, every warplane, every tank, every machine gun, every pistol, every bullet, every saber, every bayonet—all consumed by a giant fire until nothing is left but ashes. We will do well to remember this as the excruciating memories of September 11 stab our souls.

Having declared the end of wars, God now speaks to us in the first person:

> "Be still, and know that I am God.
> I will be exalted among the nations,
> I will be exalted in the earth!"

—v. 10

The divine command to "Be still" intentionally recalls Moses' command to Israel at the Red Sea. Though the people stood wedged between the armies of Pharaoh and the sea, facing what appeared to be complete annihilation, Moses commanded them, "Fear not, stand firm, and see the salvation of the LORD, which he will work for you today. For the Egyptians whom you see today, you shall never see again. The LORD will fight for you, and you have only to be silent" (Exodus 14:13, 14).

"Be still" also anticipates the words of the second Moses, Christ our Lord, when he commanded the storm-tossed sea, "Peace! Be still!" (Mark 4:39)—which his hearers linked with

Psalm 46, "Be still, and know that I am God." And during these uncertain days, God's Word likewise comes to us, saying, "Be still, and know that I am God."

Has the excruciating video footage of CNN and Fox and NBC and ABC so troubled your soul that you can scarcely concentrate, let alone pray? Then "Be still," says the Lord, "and know that I am God." Turn off the television and be still. Lay aside your newspaper and be still. Take a deep breath—take your Bible in hand—and be still and know that God is God!

I don't know what lies ahead, nor do you. I pray that it will be peace. But if not—if there is war, if the unthinkable continues to happen, if mushroom clouds rise over our cities, if anthrax rains from the skies—know this:

> The LORD of hosts is with us;
> the God of Jacob is our fortress.
>
> —v. 11

God gives us himself. He gave us his only Son. He could not do more than this. And a God who does this delights to be our "strength" and our eternal "fortress."

These are our words. Affirm them out loud to God:

> Therefore we will not fear, though the earth gives way,
> though the mountains fall into the heart of the sea,
> though its waters roar and foam,
> though the mountains tremble at its swelling.
>
> —vv. 2, 3

The LORD of hosts is with us;
the God of Jacob is our fortress.

—vv. 7, 11

And lift your voice in song:

A mighty fortress is our God,
A bulwark never failing;
Our helper he amid the flood
Of mortal ills prevailing.
For still our ancient foe
Doth seek to work us woe;
His craft and power are great;
And armed with cruel hate,
On earth is not his equal.

Did we in our own strength confide,
Our striving would be losing;
Were not the right man on our side,
The man of God's own choosing.
Dost ask who that may be?
Christ Jesus, it is he,
Lord Sabaoth his name,
From age to age the same,
And he must win the battle.

And though this world, with devils filled,
Should threaten to undo us,
We will not fear, for God hath willed
His truth to triumph through us.

The prince of darkness grim,
We tremble not for him;
His rage we can endure,
For lo! his doom is sure;
One little word shall fell him.

That Word above all earthly powers,
No thanks to them, abideth;
The Spirit and the gifts are ours
Through him who with us sideth.
Let goods and kindred go,
This mortal life also;
The body they may kill:
God's truth abideth still;
His kingdom is forever.

Amen!

*From the Archbishop's address, September 12, 2001; used by permission as quoted here.

WHY?

Joni Eareckson Tada

Even the darkness is not dark to you;
the night is bright as the day,
for darkness is as light with you.
For you formed my inward parts;
you knitted me together in my mother's womb.
I praise you, for I am fearfully and wonderfully made.
Wonderful are your works;
my soul knows it very well.
My frame was not hidden from you,
when I was being made in secret,
intricately woven in the depths of the earth.
Your eyes saw my unformed substance;
in your book were written, every one of them,
the days that were formed for me,
when as yet there were none of them.
How precious to me are your thoughts, O God!
How vast is the sum of them!
If I could count them, they are more than the sand.

PSALM 139:12-18, ESV

The world will never forget September 11th, 2001, the day when terrorism rocked the United States, leaving thousands dead and injured, the buildings of the World Trade Center in ruins, and an entire corner of the Pentagon smoldering. Four large airplanes were hijacked and used as mass weapons of destruction, leaving the families of the victims reeling from the shock.

In the aftermath of this terrible tragedy, people asked, "Why?" Many wondered about the goodness of God and the problem of so much evil and suffering. Their questions reflect ours as we face our own personal crises.

We can't live with answers like "God has nothing to do with terrible tragedies" or "God can't control evil men and their actions." We cannot be stoics either, simply resigning ourselves to a new definition for "normal life" while we plod one weary foot in front of the other. People are struggling, like a friend of mine who is going blind and recently said, "I don't want to be a saint. I don't want to get to know God better. In fact, God, maybe you should get to know me better!"

And so we ask, "Why?" To question is just part of what it means to be human, what it means to be made in the image of God. Like God, we have this strong sense of justice. It forces us to press for meaning and look for answers.

Yet you don't stop the bleeding with answers. Quick answers don't reach the problem where it hurts—in the gut and in the heart. That's because the problem of suffering is not dry and abstract; the problem is not about *something* but about *Someone.* It follows that the answer, then, must not be about something but Someone.

As Dr. Peter Kreeft suggested, "When a person is suffering, that person is like a child looking up into the face of his daddy and asking, 'Why?' The child doesn't want answers or reasons why so much as to have daddy pick him up and reassure him that everything is going to be okay."

Our heartfelt plea is for assurance—Fatherly Assurance—that there is an order to reality that far transcends our problems. We need assurance that the world is not splitting apart at the seams, that it's not in nightmarish chaos, that the world, *our* world, is orderly and stable, that somehow *everything will be okay.*

God must be at the center of our suffering. What's more, he must be consummately good. He must be Daddy, personal, compassionate. This is our cry. And God, like a father, doesn't give advice—he gives himself. After all, if you are the one at the center of the universe, holding it together so it doesn't split apart at the seams, if everything moves, breathes, and has its being in you, as it says of God in Acts 17:28, you can do no more than give yourself.

So in Psalm 18, God becomes the fortress and deliverer to those who are groping for meaning. In Psalm 10, he becomes the Father of the orphaned. In Exodus 15, he becomes the

Healer to the sick. In Isaiah 9, he is the Wonderful Counselor to the confused and depressed.

God has his reasons, and they *are* good. They are right and true! But having lived for thirty-five years in a wheelchair as a quadriplegic, I'll be the first to tell you that when your heart is being wrung out like a sponge, an orderly list of "16 good biblical reasons as to why all this has happened," although true, can sting like salt in a wound.

Besides, if answers become the "end all, be all," we end up hating trials, we end up frustrated that we can't fit them into our Daytimer™. More tragically, we end up hating God; in our thinking, he has become one who has made us jump through hoops and has given us the burdensome task of try-ing to figure out how "even this" fits into a pattern for good. A technical and abstract approach to our problems will *always* end up frustrating us.

The fact remains, we cannot distance the Bible's answers from the God of the Bible. When we feel as though our lives are spinning out of control and collapsing in nightmarish chaos, we can't "go somewhere"; instead, we must go to Someone. Someone who just might be able to do something about our plight. Like the woman with the hemorrhage in Luke 8:43, 44, we want to reach out and hang onto the hem of God's robe for dear life.

Who else can we take our case to? What higher authority is there? We have no other choice than to wake up in the morn-ing *requiring* him and *desperately* needing him.

When I broke my neck in a diving accident in 1967 and I

became paralyzed from the shoulders down, I used to ask, "Why?" I asked a lot of other questions too, like "Will I ever be happy again?" and "Will I ever get out from under this burden?" and "Will I ever understand how this fits into God's plan?" Somewhere along the line, however, I realized that the questions themselves were me-focused. Even when I used to hit upon good reasons "why," like "this is making me a better person" and "this is improving my character," I realized they were me-focused. I needed the *Someone* behind it all. I needed my focus off me and on him.

When we come to God "poor in spirit" (Matthew 5:3), when we come to God saying, "I don't get it, but I realize I need you," *things change*. Like with the woman who clung to the robe of Jesus, God releases in us a new measure of strength; he imparts a greater gift of faith; he raises us up to a new plane of trust. And we can never be the same.

That God is a part of the problem of suffering may not complicate matters after all. How or to what extent he's involved in the problem is not the question. The point is, *he* is the answer, and we need him. In suffering, God does not give the blueprint, but himself. God is a God of love, and anyone who's in love gives himself. God doesn't give a list of answers; he *is* the Answer. He's not a bunch of words; he *is* the Word.

This is why, as a Christian, I see the God of the Bible show his love most compellingly through his Son crucified on a cross. Here is Jesus Christ, the Word made flesh—gouged, with nail-pierced wrists and hands nearly ripped off, spat upon, and beaten bloody. These aren't merely facts about the Son of God.

This is love poured out like wine as strong as fire, as an ancient once said. Like the blood of the paschal lamb in the Old Testament, God got messy when he smeared blood on a cross to turn people away from hellfire—which, incidentally, is the ultimate suffering. We merely experience hell's splash-over while here on earth, reminding us and warning us all that this life is not the only life there is.

And so God allows suffering between him and us so that nothing will be *between* him and us. There are no more beautiful words in the New Testament than the apostle Paul's when he writes, "Who shall separate us from the love of Christ? Shall trouble or hardship or persecution or famine or danger or sword? . . . I am convinced that neither death nor life, neither angels or demons, neither the present nor the future, nor any powers, neither height nor depth, nor anything else in all creation, will be able to separate us from the love of God that is in Christ Jesus our Lord" (Romans 8:35, 38, 39, NIV).

We will *always* keep asking why, we will always challenge God's goodness unless we understand that God, too, experienced horrible suffering. The goodness of God is most clearly evident when you see his love expressed "in Christ Jesus our Lord."

Remember, a God who loves is a God who gives himself as the answer. Are you broken? He is broken with you. Are you disappointed? Jesus couldn't get his three best friends to spend an hour in prayer with him. Does he descend into your hell? Yes, for though the darkness is all around you, the darkness is not dark to him (see Psalm 139:11, 12).

God reveals himself through the dust and debris, the smoke

and sadness of the events of September 11, 2001. President Bush said in his message to the congregation gathered at the National Cathedral three days after the horrific events, "Adversity introduces us to ourselves." What do you find in your heart when faced with personal tragedy? What does adversity reveal to you about yourself and about your belief in God?

The Lord may not spread before you the blueprint, explaining his plans and purposes. Rather, he invites you to come to him by faith. Most, if not all, of God's answers are found at Calvary. Begin by dropping to your knees before the cross of Christ, laying all your questions at Jesus' feet. Yield any stiff-necked, stubborn rebellion—call it sin, if you will— that you might have toward him. In so doing, you'll discover the answer that will suffice for all your hurts.

It is Christ who, with his blood, has paid the penalty of his own Father's judgment against your personal evil; and as you yield your life, it is Christ who will strengthen your faith. Despite all your unanswered questions, you will receive the goal of your faith—the salvation of your soul (1 Peter 1:9). What freedom, what peace! Ask him to forgive your doubts and fears and any sin that separates you from him. Then rise in faith and move forward into your life through faith in the One who gave his life for you, the One who works all things together for your good and his glory.

That's the only Answer that ultimately matters.

THREE

OUR STEADY HOPE

John Piper

Who will separate us from the love of Christ? Will tribulation, or distress, or persecution, or famine, or nakedness, or peril, or sword? Just as it is written, "For Your sake we are being put to death all day long; we were considered as sheep to be slaughtered." But in all these things we overwhelmingly conquer through Him who loved us. For I am convinced that neither death, nor life, nor angels, nor principalities, nor things present, nor things to come, nor powers, nor height, nor depth, nor any other created thing, will be able to separate us from the love of God, which is in Christ Jesus our Lord.

ROMANS 8:35-39, NASB

When the pastoral staff of the church I pastor met within minutes after the first strikes against the World Trade Center, we put the radio in the middle of the table. We listened and turned it off and prayed and listened and prayed—and then planned. The short-term plan was three services under one title: "Sorrow, Self-humbling, and Steady Hope in our Savior and King, Jesus Christ." In addition we would immediately make a new roof banner for the church that said, "Christ, When All Is Shaking."

In that Tuesday night's service we focused on sorrow. Wednesday night we focused on self-humbling. The following Sunday morning we focused on our steady hope in our Savior and King, Jesus Christ.

So how shall I strengthen your hope?

Shall I try to strengthen your hope *politically* and assure you that America is durable and will come together in great bipartisan unity and prove that the democratic system is strong and unshakable?

Shall I try to strengthen your hope *militarily* and assure you that American military might is unsurpassed and can turn back any destructive force against the nation?

Shall I try to strengthen your hope *financially* and assure you that there will be stability and long-term growth to pre-serve the value of all your investments?

Shall I try to strengthen your hope *geographically* and assure you that you probably live far from the major political and military and financial targets that enemies might choose?

Shall I try to strengthen your hope *psychologically* and send you to the web page titled "Self-care and Self-help Following Disasters" so you can read there that "individuals with strong coping skills . . . maintain a view of self as competent . . . and avoid regretting past decisions"?

Should I try to strengthen your hope *eschatologically* by assuring you that you won't be on the earth anyway when the blazing fireball comes near your town?

The answer to those six questions is very easy for me: No! I will not try to strengthen your hope in those six ways. And the reason I won't is also very simple. None of them is true.

The American *political* system is not imperishable.

The American *military* cannot protect us from every destructive force.

The *financial* future is not certain and you may lose your investments.

No area of our nation is safe from the next kind of terrorism, which may be more pervasive and more deadly.

The *psychological* efforts to feel competent and avoid regret are not healing, but fatal.

And *eschatological* scenarios that promise escape from suffering under God's end-time providence didn't work for the

Christians in the World Trade Center on September 11, and they won't work for you either.

YOU SHOULD FEEL MORE VULNERABLE
THAN YOU ALREADY DO

So I will not contradict my calling as a minister of the Gospel by trying to strengthen your hope in those ways. Instead I want to strengthen your hope first by making sure that you feel more vulnerable than you already do in the face of the terrorism at the World Trade Center and the Pentagon.

There are two reasons for doing this. One is that we *are* more vulnerable than we think we are. The next phase of terrorism will probably not be a replay of the strategy of September 11. Instead it may be, and could be, an act of chemical warfare that unleashes deadly gas or poisons a city's water supply, just to name a couple of realistic possibilities. This would mean not five thousand dead, but hundreds of thousands dead. Perhaps millions. So we are more vulnerable than we think we are.

The second reason for sobering you in this way is that the kinds of sufferings that the Bible depicts for the people of God are far more extensive than what happened last week. Perhaps it will take this kind of calamity to help us read the Scriptures for what they are really saying and make us less secure with earthly things so we can be more secure in our Savior and King, Jesus Christ. For example, 1 Peter 4:12-19 says:

> Beloved, do not be surprised at the fiery ordeal among you, which comes upon you for your testing, as though some

strange thing were happening to you; but to the degree that you share the sufferings of Christ, keep on rejoicing, so that also at the revelation of His glory you may rejoice with exultation. If you are reviled for the name of Christ, you are blessed, because the Spirit of glory and of God rests on you. Make sure that none of you suffers as a murderer, or thief, or evildoer, or a troublesome meddler; but if anyone suffers as a Christian, he is not to be ashamed, but is to glorify God in this name. For it is time for judgment to begin with the household of God; and if it begins with us first, what will be the outcome for those who do not obey the gospel of God? . . . Therefore, those also who suffer according to the will of God shall entrust their souls to a faithful Creator in doing what is right (NASB).

So the way I want to strengthen your hope is not by glossing over how utterly vulnerable we are in our earthly existence, or by deflecting your attention away from the biblical truth that God's judgments fall on believer and unbeliever alike—purifying in some cases and punishing in other cases, depending on whether we repent and make Christ our Treasure instead of the idols of this world. I want to stare those realities of vulnerability and judgment square in the face with you and give you real, solid, biblical hope. Not just hopeful feelings based on näive notions of earthly stability or escape from painful, purifying, disciplinary judgments.

So then, what is this hope and what is the basis for it? I'll give you my answer, and then show you where I got it from the Word of God.

Our hope is that nothing can separate us from the love of God in Jesus Christ, not suffering and not even death.

And the two foundations for this hope are the death of Jesus and the sovereignty of God.

Our Savior and King, Jesus Christ, died and rose again to bear our sins, become our curse, endure our condemnation, remove our guilt, and secure our everlasting joy in the presence of the all-satisfying God.

And the sovereignty of God over all persons and events guarantees that what Jesus Christ bought for us by his own blood will infallibly become our inheritance.

Now let's go to our text and see these things in the Word of God.

OUR STEADY HOPE: NOTHING CAN SEPARATE US FROM THE LOVE OF CHRIST

First, what is our hope in the best and worst of times? When all around our soul gives way? Our hope is that nothing can separate us from the love of God in Christ, not even suffering and death. Our hope is not for an easy or comfortable or secure life on this earth. Our hope is that the love of God will grant us joy in the all-satisfying glory of God, which will continue through death and increase for all eternity.

> Who will separate us from the love of Christ? Will tribulation, or distress, or persecution, or famine, or nakedness, or peril, or sword? Just as it is written, "For Your sake we are being put to death all day long; we were considered as sheep

to be slaughtered." But in all these things we overwhelmingly conquer through Him who loved us. For I am convinced that neither death, nor life, nor angels, nor principalities, nor things present, nor things to come, nor powers, nor height, nor depth, nor any other created thing, will be able to separate us from the love of God, which is in Christ Jesus our Lord.

ROMANS 8:35-39, NASB

Your steady, solid hope—and it is the only lasting hope—is that if you will trust Christ as your precious Savior and your supremely valued King, then you will be folded into the love of God in a way that no terrorist, no torture, no demons, no disasters, no disease, no man, no microbe, no government, and no grave can destroy. That's the hope of this text. That's the hope of the Christian life. It is not a political hope, or a military hope, or a financial hope, or a geographical hope, or a psycho-logical hope, or an escapist hope. It is a blood-bought, Spirit-wrought, Christ-exalting, God-centered, fear-destroying, death-defeating hope.

And what is the foundation for this?

First Foundation of Our Hope: The Death of Christ for Us

The first answer is the death of Jesus in our place. Look at verse 32: "He who did not spare His own Son, but delivered Him over for us all, how will He not also with Him freely give us all things?" The basis of our hope that God will freely give us all we need to be satisfied in him forever is that he did not spare his own Son, but gave him for us all. He *gave* him. *For* us. God did this. And he did it for us. And verse 32 says *that* death is the foundation of our hope that he will give us every-thing that we need to be satisfied in him forever.

I say it like that—he will give us *everything we need to be sat-isfied* in the love of God forever—because what becomes clear in verse 35 is that the sovereignty of God does not guarantee our escape from suffering. It does not guarantee that we won't be in a hijacked plane or in a World Trade Center or that we won't drink the poisoned water or breathe the deadly gas. "Who will separate us from the love of Christ? Will tribulation, or distress, or persecution, or famine, or nakedness, or peril, or sword?" These words cover virtually every kind of possible calamity. "Distress" and "peril" are broad, general words for dangers of all kinds. Christians are vulnerable to all of them. If your hope is to escape them, your hope is unfounded.

And I don't want to give you unfounded hope but founded hope. The Christian hope is not that we escape these things, but that they cannot separate us from the love of God in Christ.

Second Foundation for Our Hope: The Sovereignty of God over Us

They cannot, first, because Christ paid his life to secure us for himself forever. And the second reason nothing can separate us from the love of God—the second foundation for our hope—is that God is sovereign. And the sovereignty of God over all per-sons and events guarantees that what Jesus Christ bought for us by his own blood will infallibly become our inheritance.

Where do I see that in the text? Consider verse 36: "Just as it is written, 'For your sake we are being put to death all day long; we were considered as sheep to be slaughtered.'" Now that is a quotation from Psalm 44:22. Paul quotes it for the same reason I preach the way I preach. I learned it from him. He wants to make clear, with biblical authority, that the Christian hope is not to escape slaughter. Christian hope is not to be kept off the hijacked plane or out of the collapsing building.

And this is not because God is not sovereign over all persons and events—governing all things for his own purposes (Ephesians 1:11). Why do I say this? Because when you go back and read Psalm 44, what you read is that God is not standing helplessly by while his people are counted as sheep to be slaughtered. He is handing them over to this suffering. Verses 10-13, 19 read:

> You [God] cause us to turn back from the adversary. . . . You give us as sheep to be eaten and have scattered us among the nations. You sell Your people cheaply. . . . You make us a reproach to our neighbors, a scoffing and a derision to those around us. . . . You have crushed us in a place of jackals and covered us with the shadow of death.

So when Paul says in effect in Romans 8:36, "We are being counted as sheep to be slaughtered," he does not mean that God has lost control of his world or his people. He does not mean, therefore, that God can have no holy purposes or gracious plans or merciful intentions or bright designs in this dark and dreadful and God-ordained suffering.

No. What he means is that God, who in his sovereignty hands us over to calamity, will use that very sovereignty to make life and death and angels and principalities and things present and things to come and powers and height and depth and every created thing serve our everlasting joy in God.

Oh, in the coming days of trouble may God grant you sweet sorrow and self-humbling and steady hope in our suffering Savior and sovereign King, Jesus Christ. May the Lord keep you in perfect peace, your mind being stayed on him, because you trust in him. "Trust in the LORD forever, for the LORD GOD is an everlasting rock" (Isaiah 26:3, 4, RSV).

FOUR

Gospel Comfort and Gospel Warning

Joseph "Skip" Ryan

Fear not, for I am with you;
be not dismayed, for I am your God;
I will strengthen you, I will help you,
I will uphold you with my righteous hand.

ISAIAH 41:10, ESV

In the background of chapters 12 and 13 of the Gospel of Luke are some events that in their own day and in their own way were not unlike the catastrophes we experienced on September 11, 2001. To be sure, what we have experienced is much, much greater in terms of proportions, the numbers of people killed and injured, and the public nature of the calamity; but the degree of difference is a degree of amount, not of kind. The issues are somewhat the same, and we are not told a great deal about these issues in chapter 13.

Apparently there were some Jews from Galilee, the area in northern Israel, who were in Jerusalem for a time of worship. Pilate had them killed while they were worshiping, and he somehow mixed their blood with the blood of the sacrifices that they themselves were offering in their worship—a gruesome and awful display on Pilate's part. It makes us think of the kind of racial hatred or ethnic cleansing we see in our day. Perhaps that was in Pilate's mind. It's a little like what happened in Ft. Worth two years ago when a bad and mad person came into a church service and started shooting.

These people were saying to Jesus in chapter 13, "What do you think of this, Jesus? Tell us what you say is going on here." Questions were put to Jesus that were not unlike the questions that you and I, perhaps even legitimately, have. How could God let this happen? Is he sovereign? Is he truly never for one moment out of control of the universe? How could God be sovereign and let what happened on Tuesday, September 11 happen? If God is sovereign, how could he let such wicked men loose to do their wickedness upon others?

Have you ever noticed that the Bible never answers your questions in quite the way you ask them? That is really surprising, but it is nevertheless a very important signal and pointer for us all. We want Jesus to answer us according to the precise definition and syntax of the questions we have posed to him, but Jesus says something totally unexpected. On this occasion he responded with a question that made a point and then made a point that raised a question.

QUESTIONS THAT MAKE A POINT

Jesus asked his questioners, "Do you think these Galileans were worse sinners than all the other Galileans because they suffered this way?" He dealt quickly and directly with the question. In effect, they were asking, "When bad stuff happens to people, does it mean they are bad?" Jesus dismissed that viewpoint immediately. He said, "I tell you no!" This was very emphatic.

Then Jesus made a point about an event that seems to have been well-known at the time. Eighteen people had died in the collapse of the Tower of Siloam. When Jesus was asked if these people who had died were more guilty than all the others on whom the tower didn't fall, he again made the negative point, "Absolutely not!"

A positive question should be ringing in our hearts right now. What is his positive point? Jesus begins to move to the heart of our questions and our concerns by telling us how to respond to terror and tragedy both in our individual lives—in our own individual heartaches and illnesses—and in the heartaches of our common life together as a community, and even as a nation, even in the kinds of horrors like those of September 11.

Jesus begins to move toward answers that he wants us to know, even if we're not at first raising the right questions. His answers raise questions that we should be asking. That's what Jesus is teaching us here.

SEEING THE CONTEXT

Some of you have Palm Pilots, and some of you are very proud of your Palm Pilots. When it comes time to schedule a meeting, you pull it out and schedule the meeting. Some of you even have Palm Pilots that talk to other people's Palm Pilots. I, for one, have a big old black notebook. It has the last twenty years of my life well contained in it, and it has the next twenty years of my life well planned out in it. I like my black notebook, thank you very much.

One thing about Palm Pilots that is really interesting is what someone was actually bragging to me about the other day when he was trying to convince me that I should get one. He said, "Look, Skip, you're a preacher, and you want to have a Bible with you all the time, don't you? All you have to do is whip out your Palm Pilot, boom, and there is the verse you want to read right there. The whole Bible can be contained on your Palm Pilot."

I like technology as much as the next fellow, and, yes, I'll probably get a Palm Pilot one of these days. But I'm not going to put the Scripture on it, and I'll tell you why. The problem is, when you open your Palm Pilot to a verse, what do you see? All you see is that verse. But there's more going on than that verse, and you need to see it in a context. When you have the Bible open in front of you and your eyes begin to move around the pages, you begin to see that there is more going on than simply that one verse. You begin to understand the meaning of that verse in a larger context, and it is that larger context about which Jesus was speaking in these two chapters of Luke that must be brought to bear upon the questions that we have about the particular nature of the recent tragedies themselves.

The editors of the *New International Version* put a heading at the start of Luke 12, "Warnings and Encouragements." That is a good heading because that is what these chapters are about—warnings and encouragements. We need to appreciate both. In fact, as Jesus answered the questions that he wants us to raise, he moved back and forth in these chapters from comfort to warning, from warning to comfort.

Jesus was not a very good preacher here by our standards. Preachers are told that if they want to make a point, they are supposed to make one point at a time. "Here is the point about warning." "Good, Jesus, we got that one." "Now here's the point about encouragement." "Now we get that one."

But Jesus did not teach the way we would expect him to. He moved back and forth in a way that surprises us, but you have to appreciate the whole, and so I urge you to read all of chapters 12 and 13. I think you'll find it very helpful, because what you will see is that Jesus began to answer the questions that we have about horror and tragedy and even terrorism with words of comfort.

THE BASIS OF OUR HOPE

Upon what do we base our understanding of what comfort is supposed to look like? There is a tremendous model that is sewn into the fabric and heart of the universe about comfort. There is a lesson and a moral about comfort that goes to the very heart of everything that we Christians believe. If you are a Christian believer, the right place to begin your understanding of the tragedies of September 11 is with the doctrine of the Incarnation. The Incarnation is what teaches us that God comes to comfort us. God comes in flesh. He moves into our world in the fleshness of humanity; he becomes like one of us in order to comfort us. So, for example, in Hebrews we read this marvelous statement about the nature of the Incarnation and particularly what the nature of this comfort is: The Son of God moves toward us.

> Since the children have flesh and blood, he too shared in their humanity so that by his death he might destroy him

who holds the power of death—that is, the devil—and free those who all their lives were held in slavery by their fear of death. For surely it is not angels he helps, but Abraham's descendants. For this reason he had to be made like his brothers in every way, in order that he might become a merciful and faithful high priest in service to God, and that he might make atonement for the sins of the people.

HEBREWS 2:14-18, NIV

There is so much in that passage, but note this: The comfort God gives is not abstract. The comfort God gives is not at first "spiritual." It's very fleshy. It's the comfort of touch; it's the comfort of humanity; it's the comfort of God coming in the flesh for us. It is the comfort that comes from knowing that God cares. He knows, and he weeps.

For example, John 11:33-35 (NASB) tells us:

When Jesus therefore saw her weeping, and the Jews who came with her also weeping, He was deeply moved in spirit and was troubled, and said, "Where have you laid him?" They said to Him, "Lord, come and see." Jesus wept.

Luke 19:41 (NASB) says, "When He approached Jerusalem, He saw the city and wept over it."

Psalm 34:18 (NASB) declares, "The LORD is near to the brokenhearted and saves those who are crushed in spirit."

And Isaiah 41:10 (RSV) proclaims, "Fear not, for I am with you. Be not dismayed, for I am your God; I will strengthen you, I will help you, I will uphold you with my victorious right hand."

Dear friends, I must be honest with you as a Christian preacher and say that these words are all so much thin air, meaning nothing, if it were not for the Incarnation. It is because of the Incarnation that God is with us. It is in the enfleshment of Jesus as the Son of God come into our midst that he comes, that he weeps, that he cares, that he touches. Our own rightful sense of our common humanity and the care and concern we have for our fellow human beings, no matter their religion or background, comes from the heart of God.

He not only cares, but he moves in care toward those whom he loves.

The beginning point for a response to what happened on September 11 is the enfleshment of God in this world. Jesus' first response was not to talk about whose sin caused Pilate's ethnic cleansing or whose sin caused the Tower of Siloam to fall. His first response was to talk about birds and how he cares for them. So, does he not care for you?

Dorothy Sayers, the British writer, talked about the Incarnation this way:

> For whatever reason God chose to make man as he is, limited in suffering and subject to sorrows and death, He, God, had the honesty and the courage to take His own medicine. He can exact nothing from man that He has not exacted from Himself. He has gone through the whole of human experience, from the trivial irritations of family life and the cramping restrictions of hard work and the lack of money, to the worst horrors of pain and humiliation, defeat, despair, and death. When God played the man, He played the man.

God in Christ knows what 110 stories of crushing steel and glass feel like.

Perhaps you have heard the story about the little boy who is trying to go to sleep but is scared of a noise outside. His father goes in to comfort him and says, "Let's pray to Jesus so you won't be afraid."

The little boy says, "Sure, Dad, but actually I was hoping for someone who has skin on him!"

The father wisely and rightly responds, "That's just the point, child. The Son of God has skin on him."

That is a startling thought. Do you know why you can pray to a God who understands all of the tragic failures, all the hurts and agonies of our sinful flesh? Because Jesus still has flesh. We are treading close to a wonderful line of mystery here. It is magnificent. I want to be careful, but I do not think it is too much to say that the risen, exalted, ascended Christ who is sitting at the right hand of God has skin on him right now. He knows, and he cares.

THE IMPULSE TO JUDGE

I want to make a negative point very carefully, because I want to say it in a way that is clearly understood. I cannot be honest as a pastor if I do not speak to a recent article in the *Dallas Morning News* about a preacher laying blame for the World Trade Center attack. Here is what that preacher said:

> The abortionists have got to bear some burden for this, because God will not be mocked, and when we destroy 40 million lit-

tle innocent baby lives, we make God mad. I really believe
that the pagans and the abortionists, and all the feminists, and
all the gays and lesbians who are actively trying to make that
an alternative lifestyle, the ACLU, the People for the American
Way, all of them who have tried to secularize America, I point
the finger in their face, and I say, "You helped this happen."

He went on to say that such people's actions have turned
God's anger on America. Dear friends, doctrine is very important, and that preacher's statement is very poor doctrine. It is
the wrong starting place. It is not where the Son of God starts.
Oh, I hold no brief for abortionists, and you know as well as I
do that judgment will come one day, and then the chaff will
be separated from the grain and will be burned. But the
impulse of Christian doctrine in a situation like terrorist attacks
and many violent deaths is not the impulse to judge; it is the
impulse to come alongside. For this one preacher or any
preacher to pick judgment as his doctrinal beginning point is
like a surgeon grabbing an ax as his instrument when beginning
an operation.

One of the names for the Holy Spirit is *Paraclete*. That is
the origin of words like *parallel*. It means to come alongside.
What does the Holy Spirit do? He comes alongside.

WORDS OF WARNING

Jesus gives warnings as well as comfort in these passages from
Luke. In what direction does he aim his warning? Does he
aim it toward all those bad people in our society who have

somehow brought God's judgment upon us? Does he even first aim his warning at the perpetrators of the terror that was caused in Jerusalem? The answer is an emphatic no. He first aims his warning squarely at your heart and mine.

This is where Jesus introduced the question of judgment, but he did it in a most particular way. In chapter 13 he said in effect, "You want me to pronounce judgment on Pilate for his wicked and murderous acts, but Pilate is not here. Leave Pilate to me. I'll take care of Pilate. He's not here, but you are here, and you need to see that judgment doesn't begin out there. Judgment begins in *your* hearts."

What is so disturbing about the *Dallas Morning News* article is not that America will be judged. What is so disturbing is that that preacher who says America will be judged does not candidly tell you he will be judged first. Any true Christian who understands the meaning of what God is all about in all of this must first say, "What is in my heart? What is the terrorism that is in my own heart? What is the terror of sin that has caused me to be the kind of person that I am?"

You say, "Wait a minute, Skip. I didn't fly any jet planes into buildings." I know you didn't, but I want you to know on the basis of the Word of God that the evil that lurks in men's hearts is a matter of degree, not of kind. One reason that God would even permit such wicked things to happen is so men and women, believers and nonbelievers, would have forced into their reckoning the question, "What is in my own heart?"

You know the line from John Donne's famous essay, "For Whom the Bell Tolls": "Ask not for whom the bell tolls; it tolls for thee." What you may not realize without the context of this line is that he is saying that when the bell rings, it is an alarm that must first be heard by you. He ends the poem this way: "If by this consideration of another's danger, I take mine into contemplation, then I should secure myself by making my resource to God who is our only security."

Jesus is saying, "Look at this horrible tragedy. Yes, use all the means of military and political might to do what world powers must do to cope with such awful acts. But first contemplate the meaning of this event in your own heart. Ask God to reveal the terrorism of sin that is there."

The great English writer G. K. Chesterton was once asked by the *London Times* to write an article on the question, "What is the problem of the universe?" He wrote back very concisely, "I am. Sincerely, G. K. Chesterton."

If there were a scale from zero to 100 of relative goodness for every human being, where would you put Mother Theresa? About 95? Where would you put the perpetrators of the horrors of September 11? Let's just say 1. (You probably want to put them off the scale completely.) Where would you put yourself? Most of us would put ourselves somewhere in between. What's the problem with the scale? The problem is that the difference between 99.99999999 and 100 is an infinite distance, and there is only one Man who has bridged that gap; there is only one Person who has ever worn flesh and who has ever lived perfectly, and therein lies your hope.

Did Jesus die for the terror in your heart? Yes, he died for your sins. But I want you to understand this, my friends—he not only died for your sins, he lived for your righteousness. He lived the perfect life in the flesh that you could never live. He was the Perfect One who never did, thought, or said anything—anything!—that dishonored the name of his Father; when he died on that cross of Calvary, he bestowed upon you not only the merit of his perfect death, but the merit of his perfect life.

ANSWERS TO HIS QUESTIONS

Flesh. You are robed in it, and it is full of tatters unless you are wearing the righteousness of Christ won for you. This is where we are. No, Jesus does not answer our questions just the way we ask them. He answers questions we do not ask and then makes us ask questions we did not intend to ask, but by his sovereign Spirit he brings us to the right place. We then start asking the right questions: "Who am I?" "What is my sin?" "What is the terror in my own heart?"

Then he would have us pray something like this:

Nothing in my hand I bring.
Simply to thy cross I cling;
Naked, come to thee for dress;
Helpless, look to thee for grace;
Foul, I to the Fountain fly;
Wash me, Savior, or I die.

FIVE

Where Was God on September 11, 2001?

Joseph M. Stowell

The steadfast love of the LORD never ceases;
his mercies never come to an end;
they are new every morning;
great is your faithfulness.

LAMENTATIONS 3:22, 23, ESV

September 11, 2001 will be indelibly seared into our minds and emotions for the rest of our lives. For over 5,000 families it's not just the memory that haunts them but the wrenching loss of loved ones. It is hard to imagine how anyone could participate in and perpetrate such a senseless and evil crime against harmless civilians. Throughout the week following the disaster a myriad of questions were posed about the tragedy. But none were more troubling than the questions about God: "Where was he?" "If he is a loving God, how could he let this happen?" "Does he care?" Many such inquiries begged for answers.

Thankfully there are answers. And those of us who choose to flee to God in an hour like this find refuge and solace in what we know about him and in his sufficient and abundant grace to help us in our time of need.

The Psalmist said, "Be still, and know that I am God" (Psalm 46:10, NIV). What is there that we know about him and ourselves that can bring stillness and peace to our souls and sanity and stability to our minds at a time like this?

God is. There is a God who throughout history has been intimately concerned about the affairs of men. As Creator and Redeemer he is not unaware of what happened on September 11, nor is he unconcerned. He is not responsible for what happened on that dark Tuesday. This is the kind of scheme that the one who "prowls around like a roaring lion looking for someone to devour" is responsible for (1 Peter 5:8, NIV). God created Eden, and from the beginning the intention of Satan has been to disrupt and destroy what God in his glory has created (see Genesis 3).

God is transcendent. God is vastly bigger than we are, and his wisdom expands far beyond the borders of our own limited and finite capacity to grasp all that he is and does. Our brains aren't big enough to get all the way around him. To conclude that he is unwise or unworthy at a time like this assumes that we can be his judge and that we have enough facts at our disposal to draw a final conclusion about him. Certainly he could have intervened and stopped the evil. He has done that before in history. But in this instance he didn't, and for now we don't know why. What we do know is that he is a just and loving God and cannot be unfaithful to himself. This means that ultimately justice will be done, wrongs will be made right, and love will conquer and prevail. When we don't fully understand him, we can find solace in trusting him. As Paul wrote, "Who has known the mind of the Lord? Or who has been his counselor? . . . For from him and through him and to him are all things. To him be the glory forever! Amen" (Romans 11:34-36).

God is sovereign. He is in the process of managing all of history, both the evil and the good, toward a glorious end. This heinous attack didn't throw heaven into a frenzy. There are no contingency plans in God's war room. As hard as it may seem to us now, the day will come when we will understand how this fits into his overall scheme as he ultimately defeats the forces of evil. God's Word assures us, "Then the end will come . . . after he has destroyed all dominion, authority and power. For He must reign until he has put all his enemies under his feet. The last enemy to be destroyed is death" (1 Corinthians 15:24-26, NIV).

God gave man the capacity to choose good or evil. God in his infinite wisdom created an environment for mankind in which people have a choice to love and surrender to him or to go their own way and live life on their own terms. This, then, holds the possibility of an environment where both good and evil could exist. His only other option would have been to create everyone as mechanical beings preprogrammed to act out his scheme. It would be a world without love, feeling, romance, friendships, ideas, or dreams. It would be a world where relating to our Creator would be a wooden and sterile experience. He chose rather to create a race with whom he could have a loving relationship. A scheme where he could be our God and we could be his people. The fact that man has abused the privilege of choice in order to perpetrate evil is an abuse of God's good plan.

God is love. In spite of our sin, God didn't leave us to swing in the wind of our own foolish and destructive choices. Separated from him by our choice to defy his will and his ways, we are guilty before him and are liable for eternal judgment. Unable to help ourselves, God stepped into time and space on our planet in the person of Jesus Christ. His ultimate purpose was to die in our place so that our sins and sinfulness could be covered by his love and so that even the worst of us could be forgiven and restored to him (John 3:16). Paul wrote, "But God demonstrates his own love for us in this: While we were still sinners, Christ died for us" (Romans 5:8, NIV).

God feels our pain. One of the worst attacks on decency and innocence happened two thousand years ago when Jesus, the Son of God, was mercilessly killed in the public square on a cruel cross. In a sense his death was a terrorist attack by hell against heaven. God knows what it means to suffer unjustly and to watch the horror of his own Son dying a slow and painful death. It's no wonder that Scripture tells us that Jesus is touched by the feelings of our infirmities and as such will be generous with grace and mercy to help us in our time of need (Hebrews 4:14-16).

God is patient. Instead of bringing immediate judgment on a world that offends him in overtly sinful ways, he has spanned all of history with his patience. As Lamentations 3:22-23 (NIV) says, "His compassions never fail. They are new every morning." In real history he came to repair the breach that sin had created, rather than carrying out immediate retribution. As Jesus himself said, "For God did not send his Son into the world to condemn the world, but to save the world through him" (John 3:17, NIV). And while judgment day will eventually come, Scripture affirms that the Lord "is patient with you, not wanting anyone to perish, but everyone to come to repentance" (2 Peter 3:9, NIV).

Life is uncertain. As we watched the World Trade Center towers collapse, the real pain came when we realized that people were dying by the thousands in terror and horror. People got up that morning not imagining that would be their last day on earth. We live as though we are bulletproof, as though life will go on forever, as though there will be no day of reckoning. We can rebuild the towers, but not one of the lives that was lost is coming back. How wise it would be to live each day as though it were our last day on earth. To love more, to be kind more often, to value people over possessions. "Seek the LORD while he may be found; call on him while he is near. Let the wicked forsake his way and the evil man his thoughts. Let him turn to the LORD, and he will have mercy on him, and to our God, for he will freely pardon" (Isaiah 55:6, 7, NIV).

Hate is horrible. If we learn anything from this tragedy, it must be that hate harbored in a human heart is capable of distorting the mind and producing unthinkable destruction. There is only one explanation for why these terrorists did what they did. They didn't want to take over our government, rule our land, or possess our natural resources. They hate us and our way of life. So they struck.

It should be added, it is wrong for us to hate the perpetrators of this crime against our nation. As despicable as their deed was, we dare not give them the victory of destroying our own hearts and leading us downward to become just like them. While there is a place for righteous anger against injustice, hate must not be the outcome. God has established government to preserve the safety, stability, sanity, and security of our nation. He has placed in our leaders' hands the responsibility to resist and repay those who have sought to destroy us. We need to therefore pray fervently that God will grant great wisdom to those who carry out justice against these terrorist criminals.

On a personal note, if any of us have harbored hatred in our hearts, beware. Hatred in any form is itself terrorism. It will take us places we wouldn't think of going and will do irreparable damage to homes, relationships, businesses, and our own souls. Now is the time to learn the freedom of forgiveness and the overriding benefit of living to love. After all, while we were at enmity with God he loved us all the way to the cross. As Paul wrote, "While we were still sinners, Christ died for us" (Romans 5:8, NIV).

God can turn the greatest evil into ultimate good. We have already seen much good coming from this evil attack as heroic, self-sacrificing efforts are being carried out on the streets of New York City and Washington, D.C. The unifying of our nation and the outpouring of prayer and compassion are remarkable recoveries in a country that had become far too self-serving, divided, prayerless, and compassionless. This event may just heal the wounds that we have inflicted on ourselves through decades of living to please and promote self. But ultimately God will bring even greater good as in eternity he demonstrates his deep and abiding purposes in all of this. At that moment we will marvel at his divine capacity to overrule the evil of men, and we will praise his resolve to bring justice to bear. We will bask in his love that conquers evil and makes all wrongs right.

In case you doubt that he can do this, think again. Given all the ramifications, the cross stands as a symbol of the greatest evil ever perpetrated on our planet. For three days Jesus' disciples wondered what happened to God and despaired in the confusing thought that God hadn't stopped the foolish and destructive plans of men. But three days later God turned the tables on Satan and emptied the tomb to guarantee that good would conquer evil and that life would prevail over death. It must be a very frustrating thought to Satan that even in his finest hours God still rules.

Passages to read for further thought: Psalms 2, 11, 23, 27, 46, 57; John 3:16-18; Romans 3:23; 5:8; 6:23; 8:31-39; Revelation 20:11—21:6.

SIX

LIVING BY FAITH WHEN THE WORLD IS SHAKEN

Ray Pritchard

By faith Abraham obeyed when he was called to go out to a place that he was to receive as an inheritance. And he went out, not knowing where he was going. By faith he went to live in the land of promise, as in a foreign land, living in tents with Isaac and Jacob, heirs with him of the same promise. For he was looking forward to the city that has foundations, whose designer and builder is God.

HEBREWS 11:8-10, ESV

He must have been in a hurry to get home to see his family. That's the only reason his friends could think of to explain why Thomas Burnett of San Ramon, California, changed his reservations and took an earlier flight on Tuesday morning, September 11. All his friends knew how much he loved his wife and his three daughters. No doubt he was eager to get back home from his business trip. That's why he ended up on United Airlines Flight #93 from Newark to San Francisco.

What happened next didn't surprise his friends at all. As a senior officer of a medical research firm, he was known as a take-charge leader. He had been the quarterback of his high school football team in Bloomington, Minnesota, and the president of his fraternity at the University of Minnesota. If there was a problem or a crisis, Thomas Burnett liked to face it head-on.

And that's what he did when the hijackers took over the flight. The passengers had already heard about the planes that struck the World Trade Center in New York. Sensing that they were destined for a similar fate, the male passengers decided to make a stand. Exactly what happened in the next few minutes is partly a matter of conjecture. Perhaps we will never know the full story. But we do know that Thomas Burnett called his wife with the ominous news that his flight had been hijacked. After filling her in on the details, he declared, "We're all gonna die, but three of us are going to do something." Then he added, "I love you, honey" and hung up. A few minutes later Flight #93 crashed into the woods near Pittsburgh.

Thomas Burnett was thirty-eight years old. He is survived by his wife Deena and three children—twins Madison and Halley, both five, and Anna-Claire, four.

WHAT WOULD WE HAVE DONE?

In the days since then, many of us have wondered to ourselves what we would have done if we had been on that flight. Would we have joined the others in an attempt to overpower the hijackers? Would we have risked everything, knowing we were going to die anyway?

It is sometimes said that a crisis never made any man—it only reveals what he already is. That thought is both comforting and frightening because we all wonder how we would react if everything we held dear was really on the line.

Our family.

Our health.

Our career.

Our future.

Our life.

We wonder—would we have the faith to make it? Or would we collapse? All the things we say we believe—would they still be enough when the crunch comes?

The week of September 11 was undoubtedly the longest

week any of us can remember. When the final accounting is done, the terrorist attacks on Tuesday will prove to be the single bloodiest day in American history. More than five thousand people died in the various attacks. It may interest you to know that before that week, the single bloodiest day in American history took place September 17, 1862, at the Battle of Antietam during the Civil War when 4,700 soldiers on both sides died. On December 7, 1941, 2,388 American soldiers were killed in the attack on Pearl Harbor. And 1,465 American servicemen died on D-Day, June 6, 1944.

It is still hard to believe, isn't it? Suppose that a week before the attack someone had said to you, "This week hijackers will fly planes into the World Trade Center and destroy both towers. Another plane will be flown into the Pentagon, and another hijacked plane will crash near Pittsburgh. And Air Force One and the White House will come under a terrorist threat." The very notion would have sounded absurd. That sort of thing doesn't happen in the United States. Or so we thought.

That Tuesday morning changed everything.

As Christians we say we live by faith. But what does it mean to live by faith in a world where mighty skyscrapers crumble into dust and thousands of people suddenly die? Where is God in the midst of this unthinkable tragedy? And what does faith in God look like at the end of such a terrible week?

A PLACE CALLED UR

There are many places in the Bible where we might go to find an answer to those questions. I want to focus our thinking on a passage that I have often turned to in times of sorrow and personal crisis. How can you live by faith when the world itself seems to shake beneath your feet? In order to understand the answer to that question, I would like to focus our attention on Hebrews 11. Not the whole chapter, but on one man, Abraham. And not on his whole story, but on the record of his journey to the Promised Land. The long version of Abraham's life is given in Genesis; Hebrews gives a short summary.

Let's begin with some brief facts about Abraham. When we meet him in the Bible, he is living 4,000 years ago in a far-off place called Ur of the Chaldees on the banks of the Euphrates River, not far from the mouth of the Persian Gulf. No doubt he and his wife, Sarah, worshiped the moon-god Sin. He was a prosperous, middle-aged man, successful by any human standard. Life had been good to Abraham and Sarah. Certainly they had no reason to complain. It was at precisely this moment that God spoke to him—clearly, definitely, unmistakably. What God said would change his life—and ultimately alter the course of world history.

LIVING BY FAITH MEANS ACCEPTING GOD'S CALL WITHOUT KNOWING WHERE IT WILL LEAD

"By faith Abraham, when called to go to a place he would later receive as his inheritance, obeyed and went, even though he did not know where he was going" (Hebrews 11:8, NIV).

There is only one way to describe Ur of the Chaldees. It was a world-class city. Archaeologists tell us that in Abraham's day perhaps 250,000 people lived there. It was a center of mathematics, astronomy, commerce, and philosophy. People from outlying areas moved to Ur because they wanted to be part of that great city.

No doubt many of Abraham's friends thought he was crazy. Why would anyone want to leave Ur? Obeying God's call meant giving up his friends, his career, his traditions, his home, his position, his influence, and his country. More than that, it meant risking his health and his future on a vague promise from an unseen God to lead him to "the land I will show you" (see Genesis 12:1-3, NIV). When Abraham left Ur, he burned his bridges behind him. For him there could be no turning back. Once he left the walls of Ur, he was on his own, following God's call into the unknown.

You say, "He gave all that up?" Yes. "That's kind of strange, isn't it?" Is it?

No Guarantees

Please don't miss the point. When God calls, there are no guarantees about tomorrow. Abraham truly didn't know where he was going, didn't know how he would get there, didn't know how long it would take, and didn't even know for sure how he would know he was there when he got there. All he knew was that God had called him. Period. Everything else was up in the air.

You want a long life? So do I.

You want to rise in your profession? So do I.

You want lots of friends? So do I.

You want to live long enough to see your grandchildren playing at your feet? So do I.

There is nothing wrong with those desires. Nearly all of us feel that way. But living by faith means no guarantees and no certainty about the future. If you truly want to do God's will, sometimes you will find yourself exactly where Abraham was—setting out on a new journey that doesn't seem to make sense from the world's point of view. Hebrews 11:8 (NIV) says he "obeyed and went." There was no greater miracle in his life than that. Everything else that happened flowed from this basic decision. God called, and Abraham obeyed. That truth was the secret of his life. He stepped out in faith even though there were no guarantees about his own personal future.

Their Last Football Game

Let's rewind the clock to Monday night, September 10, in New York City.

Thousands of people were watching the Monday night football game between the New York Giants and the Denver Broncos. On Tuesday morning many of the New York fans who rode the subway to work discussed with their friends the rather dismal performance of the Giants the night before. Many of those fans eventually made their way to the World Trade Center to begin a new day's work. Little did they know they had watched their last football game. They had no idea what was about to happen.

At 8:45 A.M. a plane slammed into the north tower of the World Trade Center. Shortly after 9 A.M. another plane slammed into the south tower of the World Trade Center. Hundreds died immediately. Thousands would die when the towers collapsed not long later.

Among the passengers on the first plane to hit the World Trade Center was Jeff Mladenik, an associate pastor of Christ Church in Oak Brook, Illinois, a Chicago suburb. His particular calling was to find ways to encourage Christians to live out their faith boldly and creatively in the marketplace. That is a noble and much-needed ministry in our day. We might ask a few questions at this point. Was his faith weak? No. Had he sinned? No. Was he somehow out of God's will? No. Did God make a mistake? No. Did God break his promise? No. Did Jeff plan to die that day? Absolutely not. Pastor Mladenik was in the will of God when he boarded that plane, and he was in the will of God when he died in the crash.

It is good to recall what soldiers are told before a battle begins: "You have to go. You don't have to come back." The same is true for the soldiers in the army of the Lord. When Christ calls, we have to go. We don't have to come back.

Living by faith means stepping out for God and leaving the results to him. It does not guarantee a long life or good success. You may have either or both. But you may not. The life of faith means, "I am going to be the man or woman God wants me to be, no matter where that leads. I don't know the future, but I'm trusting him to work out the details. In the meantime I step out by faith and follow where he leads me."

LIVING BY FAITH MEANS WAITING FOR GOD TO KEEP HIS PROMISES

"By faith he made his home in the promised land like a stranger in a foreign country; he lived in tents, as did Isaac and Jacob, who were heirs with him of the same promise" (Hebrews 11:9, NIV).

There is within all of us a natural desire to settle down. The older I get, the less I like to move, and the more I value coming home to the same place and the same faces every day. Moving has a way of making us feel unsettled, uprooted, and adrift in the world. Multiply that feeling by a factor of 100 and spread it out over fifty years and you approximate Abraham's situation as he came to the Promised Land. Our text tells us that "he lived in tents." I know lots of people who like to camp on vacation, but I don't know anyone who voluntarily lives in a tent as a permanent residence. Tents speak of impermanence, of the possibility of moving on at any moment, of the fact that you live on land you do not personally own.

That's Abraham. He didn't own anything in the Promised Land. God had promised to give him the land; yet he lived like "a stranger in a foreign country." If you don't own the land, you can't build a permanent dwelling there. In many ways this is even more remarkable than leaving Ur in the first place. As long as Abraham was traveling across the desert, he could dream about the future. But when he got to Canaan, all illusions disappeared. Think of what he didn't find:

No "Welcome, Abraham" sign.

No discount coupons from the merchants.

No housewarming party.

No visit from the Welcome Wagon.

No mayor with the key to the city.

No band playing "Happy Days Are Here Again."

No ticker-tape parade.

Nobody expected him. Nobody cared that he had come. Nobody gave him anything.

God's Timetable . . . and Ours

God had promised him the land, but Abraham had to scratch out an existence in tents. Hundreds of years would pass before the promise was completely fulfilled. Abraham never saw it happen. Neither did Isaac or Jacob. Was Abraham in the will of God? Yes. Was he right to leave Ur? Yes. Was he doing what God wanted him to do? Yes. Why, then, was he living in tents? Because God's timetable is not the same as ours. He's not in a big hurry like we are. God works across the generations to accomplish his purposes; we're worried about which dress or shirt to buy for the big party this weekend. There is a big difference in those two perspectives.

"We Are at War"

It is a false and dangerous theology that says, "If I trust God, everything will work out fine and all my dreams will come true." Many times the very opposite seems to be the case. Too many people follow Jesus for the wrong reasons. What did you sign up for? A picnic in the park? A tea party? Jesus calls you to take up your cross daily and follow him.

Days after the attack President Bush said, "We are at war."

Do we understand what those words mean? Do we have any idea of the sacrifice that is ahead for all of us? I am sure the answer is no. Perhaps it is well that we don't know what is in store. The days ahead will not be easy. I wish I could promise that there will be no more terrorist attacks, but I can't do that. I don't doubt that there are some people who, if they had the chance, would blow up the Sears Tower in Chicago tomorrow morning. That isn't a prediction; it's simply a statement of the situation.

As we move forward, it is vitally important that we let go of anger and bitterness. This is no time to point fingers or to falsely accuse those who happen to be from a different region of the world or come from a different ethnic background. The road ahead is hard enough without descending into divisive insinuations.

We may have to live in tents for a while. Who can say what tomorrow will bring? Our challenge is to, like Abraham, cling to the promises of God no matter what happens. We may have to say at some point, "We would rather die with the Lord than live without him." In God's time every promise will be fulfilled. Meanwhile, we watch and wait and walk by faith.

There was a third principle at work in Abraham's life. It is the ultimate key to the life of faith.

LIVING BY FAITH MEANS NEVER TAKING YOUR EYES OFF HEAVEN

"For he was looking forward to the city with foundations, whose architect and builder is God" (Hebrews 11:10).

Abraham looked for a city "with foundations"—that is, for "a city," not a lonely spot in the desert. He wanted to live in a place filled with other people. He also looked for a city "with foundations," a place with security and permanence where the buildings wouldn't crumble in the middle of the morning. That meant he was looking for a city designed and built by God. Why? Because all earthly cities eventually crumble to the dust. I have visited the ruins of the ancient city of Jericho. When most people think of Jericho, they think of the city whose walls came tumbling down in the days of Joshua. But that's only one Jericho. Archaeologists have discovered layers of Jericho, one after another, the city having been built, destroyed, and rebuilt across the centuries. The same is true of Jerusalem. When you visit Old Jerusalem, you aren't exactly "walking where Jesus walked." You are actually walking thirty to seventy-five feet above where Jesus walked. According to one source, Jerusalem has been destroyed and rebuilt at least forty-seven times in the last 3,500 years. That's the way it is with all earthly cities. Nothing built by man lasts forever. We saw that firsthand when the twin towers of the World Trade Center, the very symbol of American economic power, crumbled to the ground.

No wonder Abraham was looking for a city built and designed by God. Revelation 21 describes that city as "the New Jerusalem, coming down out of heaven from God" (verse 2). In his vision John saw a city of breathtaking beauty, shining with the glory of God, "and its brilliance was like that of a very precious jewel, like a jasper, clear as crystal" (verse 11). Christians have always looked to the New Jerusalem as the final abode for the people of God, the place where we will spend eternity together in the presence of the Lord. But note this: Heaven is a city. It's a real place filled with real people. That's the city Abraham was looking for when he left Ur of the Chaldees.

Abraham was going to heaven, and he knew it. That one fact—and that alone—explains his life. He had his heart set on heaven, and that explains why he could

Leave the beautiful city of Ur.

Walk away from his career.

Leave his friends far behind.

Live in tents until the end of his life.

Start all over again in a new land.

Die without seeing all that God had promised.

Abraham knew he was going to heaven, and that changed his whole perspective on life. He knew that after death he was going to enter a city God had designed and made.

A City Built by God

What would such a city look like? It would be a city with

No pollution, for the skies would always be crystal-clear.

No crime or violence, for no criminals would ever enter.

No greedy politicians, no drug pushers, no child molesters.

No hijackers, no terrorists hiding in distant mountains.

No planes turned into flying torpedoes.

No weeping children.

No disaster relief funds.

No candlelight vigils for the dead and dying.

It would be filled with abundant parks, sparkling rivers,

rolling meadows, and flowing streams. Lining the streets would be flowers in constant bloom, fruit trees of every kind, every species of plant life—all free from pestilence and disease. The gates would be made of pearl, the walls of jasper, the streets of gold. Precious stones would lie on the ground like playthings—emeralds, rubies, diamonds galore. On every hand there would be children laughing, bright conversation, music floating from every direction.

In the city that God builds, there are no tears; there is no sorrow, no regret, no remorse. Bitterness is gone forever, failure left far behind, suffering redeemed and rewarded. There are no eyeglasses, no braces, no wheelchairs, no false teeth, and no hearing aids. There are no hospitals, no nursing homes, no paramedics, no CPR. Doctors have to find a new job—they aren't needed anymore. Aspirin is gone, accidents over, cancer disappeared, heart attacks banished, AIDS a distant memory. In heaven no one grows old and feeble.

There is one other thing you won't find in heaven. There are no cemeteries in the city God builds. Why? There are no funerals, for in that glad city no one ever dies. If you make it to that city, you live forever, never to die again. Either you believe in heaven or you don't. It's either a real place or it isn't. And it is!

FIVE LESSONS TO PONDER

Let me ask a personal question: How long do you expect to live? To put it more pointedly, how many more years do you think you have left before someone holds your funeral service? Ten years? Twenty years? Thirty years? Forty years? Fifty years?

Sixty years? How much of that time are you sure of? The last question is easy. You're not sure of any of it. The truth is, you could die tomorrow from any of a thousand causes. No one knows how long he or she will live or precisely when he or she will die. There are no guarantees for any of us. After September 11, no one can deny that fact.

Let's wrap up this message with some lessons we all should have learned from that long and difficult week when terrorists changed America forever.

Nothing in this world is secure, certain, or safe

This ought to be fully obvious to all of us. If the World Trade Center and the Pentagon are not safe, where can we hide from trouble? Many of us have lived in a self-created bubble of false security where we could watch the troubles of the world while thinking, *That could never happen to me*. No one can say that anymore.

There will be no end of evil this side of heaven

I am not a pessimist by any means, but I am a biblical realist. And although I am not a prophet, I think there may be some difficult days ahead for all of us. My advice is simple: Buckle up. The road ahead is bound to be bumpy. We will not be delivered from evil until Jesus comes again.

God can bring beauty out of the ashes of tragedy

This is the positive side of all that has happened on September 11 and the following days. Our God is so great that even a tragedy like this cannot foil his plan. We have seen angels of mercy working around the clock, digging through the rubble, searching for survivors, treating the wounded, caring for the hurting, comforting the brokenhearted, donating blood, giving money, and sending trucks filled with supplies to the disaster sites. And there has been a vast national turning to the Lord, the likes of which we have not seen in many years. The terrorists struck a blow for evil, but that is not the end of the story. "When it's sin versus grace, grace wins hands down" (Romans 5:20, Eugene Peterson, *The Message*).

There are open hearts everywhere—be bold!

This is a word of encouragement for Christians. Many of us have prayed for years for God to open the heart of our nation to the Gospel. This tragedy has changed everything. Now you can pray in the public schools and you won't get in trouble. People who before the attack were closed now want to talk about spiritual things. You can walk down the street, stop some strangers, and say, "Let's pray" and they won't laugh at you. Every head will be bowed in prayer.

The church I pastor had two evening prayer meetings after the terrorist attacks—on Tuesday and Wednesday nights. On Friday morning we got so many calls about the National Day of Prayer and Remembrance that we decided to open the sanctuary for quiet meditation at noon. Then so many more calls came in that we decided to put together a brief prayer service. At 11 A.M. we got a call from the Old Navy store located about four blocks from us. We don't know anyone there. "Are you having a service at noon?" "Yes," we said. "We'll be there." They closed the store, locked the doors, and the whole staff walked to Calvary, came in, and sat in the front of the sanctuary. I've read stories about days of long ago when stores closed for prayer meetings but never saw it happening with my own eyes until that week.

These are amazing days. As God gives you opportunity and open doors, be bold. Speak the truth in love. Millions of Americans are turning to God.

If you decide to follow Jesus, you may not be safe, but your life will never be dull

That sentence sums up everything I've been trying to say in this message. If it's safety you want and a guarantee of earthly success, you'll have to look somewhere else. But if you are willing to follow Jesus, I can promise you that you'll never be disappointed in him, and your life will not be boring.

On the Friday morning after the attack Dr. Billy Graham took part in the prayer service at the National Cathedral in Washington. He spoke powerfully and clearly, and with great compassion he pointed people to Jesus Christ as the only answer. Here is part of what he said: "There is hope for the present because I believe the stage has already been set for a new spirit in our nation. One of the things we desperately need is a spiritual renewal in this country. We need a spiritual revival in America. And God has told us in his Word, time after time, that we are to repent of our sins and to turn to him and he will bless us in a new way."

ARE YOU READY?

The challenge is always personal. The renewal we need must begin in each of us personally. There is no reason to worry about anyone else until we ourselves are right with God. After one of the services the Sunday after the terrorist attacks, a man showed me his lapel pin. It read, "Are you ready?" Good question. How many of the people who died on Tuesday, September 11, were ready to meet God? How many of us are ready right now? We are here for such a short time. Your life is like a vapor that appears for a moment and then vanishes away (James 4:14).

No one knows the future. Are you ready to meet the Lord? It is precisely at this point that the cross of Christ becomes so relevant. When Jesus died, he made the full payment for your sins so you could have a personal relationship with God. He paid the price so your sins could be forgiven and you could go to heaven. He made a way for you to have full assurance of your eternal destiny. Those who trust in him have nothing to fear at the moment of death. They are truly ready to die.

As he finished his remarks, Dr. Graham mentioned the hymn "How Firm a Foundation" and noted that all of us have a choice to make about the foundation we build our lives upon. If we build on the things of this world, we are bound to be disappointed in the end. But if we build our lives on Jesus Christ, when death comes we will discover that the foundation is firm indeed.

The week of September 11 was a terrible week, but in many ways it was also an awesome week as millions of people began looking to God in a new way. Earthly foundations were destroyed, but many people are discovering that Jesus is the firm foundation for life and for death.

One of the verses of that familiar hymn seems especially appropriate for these days:

> "Fear not, I am with thee; O be not dismayed!
> For I am thy God, and will still give thee aid;
> I'll strengthen thee, help thee, and cause thee to stand,
> Upheld by my righteous, omnipotent hand."

There may be more shaking of the foundations in the days to come. We would all be wise to build our lives on Jesus Christ. He is the one true firm foundation that can stand the test of time. Build your life on Jesus, and when the ground shakes beneath your feet and the things of the earth crumble to the ground, your life will be secure because you have built on the foundation that can never be moved. Amen.

SEVEN

A Time of Terror and a Word of Hope

Adrian Rogers

So Jesus again said to them, "Truly, truly, I say to you, I am the door of the sheep. All who came before me are thieves and robbers, but the sheep did not listen to them. I am the door. If anyone enters by me, he will be saved and will go in and out and find pasture. The thief comes only to steal and kill and destroy. I came that they may have life and have it abundantly. I am the good shepherd. The good shepherd lays down his life for the sheep.

JOHN 10:7-11, ESV

Not long ago I went to New York City to visit the World Trade Center. I stood in that plaza and looked up at those two soaring towers, gleaming with glass and steel; and as I did, my jaw almost fell to my chest. I gasped at the monumental magnificence of the work of men's hands. And yet a few days later I, like you, turned on the television and watched those towers crumble into ruins and dust, and we, as a nation, looked into the very face of evil.

September 11, 2001, will go down as the bloodiest day in American history. Those towers that represented American ingenuity and business are gone. And the Pentagon, the very symbol of American strength, had a hijacked airplane fly through it like it was a crate of eggs. We've had to think, we've had to pray as we watched fellow Americans run through ash-covered streets, fleeing for their very lives. And may God have mercy upon those who are still buried beneath a mountain of twisted steel.

One verse from God's Word puts all of this into proper perspective. John 10, verse 10 says: "The thief cometh not, but for to steal, and to kill, and to destroy" (KJV). Jesus then said, "I am come that they might have life, and that they might have it more abundantly."

First of all, I want us to recognize the ultimate reason for this time of terror. People are asking questions today. I've been interviewed by many, many radio and television stations. One man asked me bluntly the very first thing, "Where was God when all of this was going on?" I said, "Friend, I'll tell you where God was not. God was not up in heaven pacing about, wringing his hands, saying, 'What am I going to do?' God is still on the throne." Another asked this question: "Why did God do this?" May I tell you emphatically that God did *not* do this.

Satan is the ultimate terrorist. You say, "Osama bin Laden was behind it." But who was behind him? We're not wrestling with flesh and blood. Until we wake up, we'll never get a proper answer because we'll never go to the heart of the problem. Jesus told us the heart of the problem in John 10:10: "The thief cometh not, but for to steal, and to kill, and to destroy." There Jesus was speaking of Satan himself.

Now I want to say something else. This attack did not take God by surprise. God knows the wickedness of human hearts. Satan could not have done this without men's compliance. And when God made human beings, God gave them the freedom of choice. That's one of the greatest blessings and greatest dangers that we have. I've often said that human beings are free to choose, they're not free not to choose, and they're not free to choose the consequences of their choice. There are those who have collaborated with Satan. But that has not taken God by surprise.

Now some people, dewy-eyed and uninstructed in the Scriptures, think that sooner or later we are going to make this world a safe place, and there will be peace on earth, and we're going to do it by human ingenuity. And they think that the preaching of the Gospel will do that. I don't want to disillusion anyone, but I don't want anyone to have illusions either. That is not the job given to the Gospel.

The Gospel was never given to save civilization from wreckage. The Gospel is given to save men from the wreckage of civilization. And if you think for one moment that somehow we're going to bring in utopia by our own schemes and plans, you're wrong. To the contrary, listen to the Scriptures.

Second Timothy, chapter 3, verse 1, tells us: "This know also, that in the last days perilous times shall come." There are no ifs, ands, or buts about that. There's no stutter about that. There's no equivocation. "In the last days perilous times shall come." The Greek word here translated "perilous" is only used one other time in Scripture, and there it is part of a phrase translated "exceeding fierce" (Matthew 8:28). These are dangerous days. Things can happen that overwhelm us.

That Tuesday morning Joyce and I had gone for a walk. It was a beautiful morning. When we came in from the walk, we were told to turn on the television, that the World Trade Center had been hit. Let me give you the first Scripture that came to my mind: Revelation 18, beginning with verse 17: "For in one hour so great riches is come to nought. And every shipmaster, and all the company in ships, and sailors, and as many as trade by sea, stood afar off, and cried when they saw the smoke of her burning, saying, What city is like unto this great city! And they cast dust on their heads, and cried, weeping and wailing, saying, Alas, alas, that great city, wherein were made rich all that had ships in the sea by reason of her costliness!" Now listen to this phrase: ". . . for in one hour is she made desolate." This great city is in one hour made desolate. How could it be? We felt so secure.

Now this Scripture is not talking about New York City. It's talking about the Babylon to come, but oh, how graphic it is, and how it reminds us how fragile we are. These twin towers, like the ancient tower of Babel, came crumbling down. The Pentagon is the symbol of the mightiest nation this world has ever known, and yet it was vulnerable. What I'm saying to you is that God did not cause this. Satan caused it. But he could not have done it without the free choice of mankind. It did not take God by surprise. To the contrary, days like this were clearly prophesied.

Jesus said the last days would be like the days before the Flood, the time of Noah. Consider what our Savior said in Matthew 24, beginning in verse 36. He was speaking of his second coming, and he said, "But of that day and that hour knoweth no man, no, not the angels of heaven, but my Father only." No one—no one!—can set a date for the second coming of Jesus Christ. But God does tell us what the times will be like. Verse 37 says, "But as the days of Noe were, so shall also the coming of the Son of Man be. For as in the days that were before the flood they were eating and drinking, marrying and giving in marriage, until the day that Noe entered into the ark, and knew not until the flood came, and took them all away; so shall also the coming of the Son of Man be. Then two shall be in the field; the one shall be taken, and the other left. Two women shall be grinding at the mill; the one shall be taken, and the other left. Watch therefore: for ye know not what hour your Lord doth come."

Now, most of us feel that history, as we know it, is coming to a climax. What we've seen, I believe, are foreshocks and fore-gleams of Armageddon. Jesus said that if you want to be able to read the signs of the times, go back in the Scriptures and see what it was like in the days of Noah before God destroyed the world with a flood. ". . . as it was, so shall it be." I want to give you the marks of Noah's day, and I want you to consider whether they line up with our day.

First of all, *the time of Noah's day was a day of secular philosophy*. Three chapters tell us about the days of Noah—Genesis 4, 5, and 6. And Genesis 6:5 says that in the days of Noah, "God saw that the wickedness of man was great in the earth, and that every imagination of the thoughts of his heart was only evil continually." Now the word "imagination" there does not mean daydreams; it means philosophies. It comes from a Hebrew root that means to fashion something as someone would fashion a vessel. Commenting on this, John Phillips said, "Men fashioned wicked philosophies and espoused wicked causes, made fashionable vile sins, and endeavored to pour society into their mold." There's more ungodly philosophy in the world and in America than ever before.

Second, the days of Noah were *days of scientific progress*. As you read Genesis 4, 5, and 6, you'll find they were building great cities. You'll see that they had smelting furnaces. Indeed, they had great technological advances. For example, Genesis 4:17 says, "And Cain knew his wife; and she conceived, and bare Enoch: and he builded a city." And then we read in Genesis 4:22, "And Zillah . . . also bare Tubal-Cain, an instructor of every artificer in brass and iron." Industry began a long time ago, in the days of Noah. And men were thumping themselves on their big chests and saying, "Look what we have done." The same thing has happened in our nation and in our world. The Bible says that in the last days knowledge will increase and men will rush to and fro. We're so proud of our inventions, our genetic engineering, our experimentation, our moving toward a cashless society, our virtual reality, our instant communication, the worldwide net. But for the first time man is afraid of what he knows.

Third, the days of Noah were *days of sexual immorality*. Genesis 4:19 relates, "And Lamech took unto him two wives." God's plan had been one man for one woman till death do them part. Genesis 6:12 adds, "And God looked upon the earth, and, behold, it was corrupt; for all flesh had corrupted his way upon the earth." As already mentioned, Jesus said in Matthew 24:37 that they were "marrying and giving in marriage." Bible scholars tell us this speaks of a multiplicity of marriages. Furthermore, Jesus linked the days of Lot with the days of Noah. In Luke 17:26 he says, "And as it was in the days of Noe, so shall it be also in the days of the Son of man. They did eat, they drank, they married wives, they were given in marriage, until the day Noe entered the ark, and the flood came, and destroyed them all." Then he went on: "Likewise also as it was in the days of Lot; they did eat, they drank, they bought, they sold, they planted, they builded; but the same day that Lot went out of Sodom it rained fire and brimstone from heaven, and destroyed them all. Even thus shall it be in the day when the Son of Man is revealed."

God left Sodom, with its smoking ruins, as a reminder to this generation. What does God do with a generation that lives in sexual immorality? Does God step in to judge them? To the contrary, God leaves them alone, and they judge themselves. The Bible says in Romans 1, verse 26: "For this cause God gave them up unto vile affections: for even their women did change the natural use into that which is against nature." Romans 1:28 adds, "And even as they did not like to retain God in their knowledge, God gave them over to a reprobate mind." One of the worst things that God could do to any generation is just to turn them over to their sins.

Next, *the days of Noah were days of selfish indifference.* Everybody was having a party. "They were eating and drinking, marrying and giving in marriage" in the face of coming judgment. Ezekiel 16, verse 49 tells about Sodom in the same way: "Behold, this was the iniquity of thy sister Sodom, pride, fullness of bread, and abundance of idleness was in her and in her daughters, neither did she strengthen the hand of the poor and needy. And they were haughty, and committed abomination before me: therefore I took them away as I saw good." America has been living in prosperity, soaked with sin, and oblivious to the needs of so many. I can imagine that the people of Noah's day and those in Lot's day asked, "Do you think we're in trouble? Do you think perhaps judgment will come?" And others would shrug and say, "No. As a matter of fact, we're prospering quite well."

But now let's sum it up and say this: *The stunning mark of Noah's day was violence.* Listen to Genesis, chapter 6, verses 11 and following: "The earth also was corrupt before God, and the earth was filled with violence. And God looked upon the earth, and, behold, it was corrupt; for all flesh had corrupted his way upon the earth. And God said unto Noah, The end of all flesh is come before me; for the earth is filled with violence through them; and, behold, I will destroy them with the earth." Our age, similar to the time of Noah, is an age of violence, sky-jackings, kidnappings, guerrilla warfare, and needless murders. Terror now stalks the streets of every major city in this world. Organized crime may be a bigger business than the United States government. And in Noah's day there was a terrorist too. His name was Lamech. Genesis 4:23 says, "And Lamech said to his wives, Adah and Zillah, Hear my voice; ye wives of Lamech, hearken unto my speech: for I have slain a man to my wounding, and a young man to my hurt." That is, "I got in a battle. I killed a man, but he wounded me." And then this man says bitterly, "If Cain shall be avenged seven-fold, truly Lamech seventy and sevenfold." He said, "I'm going to take 77 lives for the thing that has happened to me." Here was a man who'd been hurt, and he became a violent terrorist. And in America we are seeing what the Scripture says when it says in John 10:10, "The thief cometh not, but for to steal, and to kill, and to destroy."

Now the question is this: If God did not cause this, who caused it? Satanically inspired men caused it. Could God have prohibited it? Obviously he could have; obviously he didn't. So God did not cause it, but God allowed it. Why did God allow it? He could have stopped it. So evidently, in his wisdom he had some reason to at least allow it. Let me ask this another way.

Why has this God-blessed America of ours been so God-blessed? Why is it that the pestilence and the terror and the war that have reached other shores have not reached ours? America has been blessed by God. No other nation had such a Christian beginning as America.

When our forefathers came, the pilgrim fathers, they wrote the Mayflower Compact underneath the decks of the *Mayflower*, and they said their stated purpose for coming to these shores was for the glory of God and the propagation of the Gospel of our Lord and Savior Jesus Christ. And God put a hedge around this country. Did you know that in the Bible there is a doctrine of hedges, that God can put hedges around people and individuals and nations? Let me give you an example.

God put a hedge around a man named Job. Satan tried to get to Job, but God would not allow it. Job, chapter 1, verses 9 and 10 says, "Then Satan answered the Lord, and said, Doth Job fear God for nought? Hast not thou made an hedge about him, and about his house, and about all that he hath on every side? thou hast blessed the work of his hands, and his substance is increased in the land." Satan said, "I've been trying to get at this man, but I can't get at him." Satan tried, but there was a hedge around Job.

The same was true of ancient Israel. Isaiah 5, verses 1-5 says, "Now will I sing to my wellbeloved a song of my beloved touching his vineyard. My wellbeloved [speaking of God] hath a vineyard in a very fruitful hill; and he fenced it, and gathered out the stones thereof, and planted it with the choicest vine, and built a tower in the midst of it, and also made a winepress therein: and looked that it should bring forth grapes, and it brought forth wild grapes. And now, O inhabitants of Jerusalem, and men of Judah, judge, I pray you, betwixt me and my vineyard. What could have been done more to my vineyard, that I have not done in it?"

God said, "I took this nation Israel. I planted these people. I made a vineyard. I did all that I could do for them." Now notice this: "Wherefore, when I looked that it should bring forth grapes, brought it forth wild grapes? And now go to; I will tell you what I will do to my vineyard: I will take away the hedge thereof, and it shall be eaten up; and break down the wall thereof, and it shall be trodden down."

God had put a hedge around this nation. But he said, "I gave them all they needed. I blessed them with prosperity, and I looked for fruit. But what did I get but wild grapes? I'll take down the hedge."

May I tell you why America has been so strong? America's first line of defense has not been the military, but God himself. But we have politely told God to take his hedge and go back to heaven. As a nation we've told God, "There's no room for you here in this land. Take your hedge, take your prayers, take your commandments—we'll handle things ourselves."

As a matter of fact, the Supreme Court of the United States of America said it's wrong for little children to begin their school day with a prayer. Here was the prayer that was ruled illegal in the United States on June 17, 1963: "Almighty God, we acknowledge our dependence upon Thee and beg Thy blessings upon us, our parents, our teachers, and our country." You can't pray that in schools in America! "Almighty God" is the One who has built a hedge around us, the One who has protected us.

You might say, "You know, if we mention God in the classroom, and people have the freedom to pray or carry their Bibles, somebody might be offended." Well, there's nothing in the Constitution that keeps people from being offended. And *our* children are offended every day by hearing God's name blasphemed and by hearing ungodly rock music and rap that glorifies violence, by hearing dirty words in the classroom. Our people, our children are offended by this blasphemy and filthy speech. Why are blasphemy and filthy speech protected but praise and truth are not?

What I'm trying to say is this: We must remember the reason for the problems that we have. The Bible says this is the work of Satan. Satan comes, the thief comes, to steal and to kill and to destroy. Human beings can be in compliance with Satan, but he is the master terrorist.

But we must also remember the ultimate reason for a word of hope. I'm grateful that John 10:10 has such balance. Jesus said, "The thief cometh not, but for to steal, and to kill, and to destroy: I am come that they might have life, and that they might have it more abundantly." Our Savior is not the author of death but of life.

The morning after this tragedy, I saw in bold, somber headlines the words "Evil Acts." We have seen the very face of evil. Well, take evil and spell it backwards. E-v-i-l becomes l-i-v-e. Jesus came that we might live, not die. Satan comes that we might die and not live. "The thief cometh not, but for to steal, and to kill, and to destroy. I am come," Jesus said, "that you might have life, and have it abundantly."

Our nation has been shaken to her knees. But there are some things that cannot be shaken. In Hebrews 12, beginning in verse 25, God is speaking. "See that ye refuse not him that speaketh . . ."

You see, we have a choice. God is speaking. God is shouting. "See that ye refuse not him that speaketh. For if they escaped not who refused him that spake on earth, much more shall we not escape, if we turn away from him that speaketh from heaven: whose voice then shook the earth: but now he hath promised, saying, Yet once more I shake not the earth only, but also heaven. And this word, Yet once more, *signifieth the removing of those things that are shaken, as of things that are made* . . ." (emphasis added).

God shook these mighty towers that we made, and they fell. Or rather, God allowed them to be shaken, and they fell. But notice the next word in the text—*wherefore*. Every time you see a *wherefore* in the Scripture, ask yourself, what is it there for? "Wherefore we receiving a kingdom which cannot be moved [that's just another word for shaken], let us have grace, whereby we may serve God acceptably with reverence and godly fear: for our God is a consuming fire."

Now there are things that can be shaken. Everything that man makes can be shaken. It's all premature rubble. But I want to mention three things that cannot be shaken.

God's kingdom cannot be shaken. Verse 28 says, ". . . a kingdom which cannot be moved." There is a kingdom that cannot be shaken. I had a meal one time with Corrie Ten Boom. I decided to talk very little and to listen. One thing she said I'll never forget. She said, "There's no panic in heaven, only plans." There is a kingdom that cannot be shaken.

I've read of some sailors who were shipwrecked in a stormy sea. They didn't know in which direction land was. It was nighttime. But then the clouds opened, and one sailor saw the North Star. When he saw that star, he said, "Now I know the direction to the shore." And they manned the oars and began to pull in the direction of the shore. Then one sailor said, "Keep your eye on that star, for if we lose sight of it, we're lost." I tell you, there is a star in the heavens. It is God himself, and he cannot fall.

Not only is God's kingdom not able to be shaken—*God's Word is never shaken.* Verse 25 says, " . . . him that speaketh." And verse 26 adds, "now he hath promised . . ." Thank God for that. "Forever, O Lord, thy Word is settled in heaven." I don't know about you, but when times like this come to me, I want to know, is there a word from God?

I'm not interested in what some philosopher, politician, scientist, or mathematician has to say about it. I want to know what God says. I've often said there are three categories of people in the world today—those who are afraid, those who are not afraid or who don't know enough to be afraid, and those who know their Bibles. God's kingdom can't be shaken. And God's Word cannot be shaken either.

Furthermore, *God's grace cannot be shaken.* Verse 28 says, "Wherefore . . . let us have grace." Having infinite grace, we need never be shaken.

There are two other twin towers. One is faith, the other is hope; and they stand on the foundation of the grace of God. I want to tell you that our God is a loving God. Our God wants to forgive. Our God wants to heal this land. I thank God that we can stand on God's grace. We can truthfully sing, "The soul that on Jesus hath leaned for repose, I will not, I will not desert to its foes; that soul, though all hell should endeavor to shake, I'll never, no never, no never forsake."

God's alarm clock has gone off. What time is it? What should we do?

Number one: it's a time to trust. Trust God. He will see you through. Your anchor will hold. The Scripture says, "What time I am afraid, I will trust in thee" (Psalm 56:3). There's no panic in heaven, just as Corrie Ten Boom said, only plans.

Number two: it's a time to love. Don't let your heart become a headquarters for hate. Let this terrible wickedness be the dark velvet upon which the diamond of God's love can be seen. This is an opportunity for us to show what pure religion is, to show what the grace of God is.

People, in the name of their religion, are slaughtering innocent human beings with blood and mayhem, unimaginable brutality and horror. Let that be the dark background for the love of God.

Our faith is not the faith of the sword or coercion. If you have Arab neighbors, Muslim neighbors who do not agree with this, go to them and share the love of Jesus with them. Share the love of Jesus with everybody, whether they are Jews or Gentiles, Muslims, Arabs, whites, blacks. This is a time for a mighty baptism of love. No faith, no religion that's built on mayhem and murder is of God. "The thief cometh not, but for to steal, and to kill, and to destroy." But Jesus has come that we might have life.

You might say, "Pastor Rogers, do you mean that there's not to be any military action?" Oh, there must be military action. That's why God gave us government. God told us that as individuals, we're to love. And God says, "Vengeance is mine; I will repay, saith the Lord. Therefore if thine enemy hunger, feed him; if he thirst, give him drink; for in so doing thou shalt heap coals of fire on his head. Be not overcome of evil, but overcome evil with good" (Romans 12:18-20). That's our job. That's our duty as the church, as Christians.

But in the very next chapter, Romans 13, verses 3 and 4, God says, "For rulers are not a terror to good works, but to the evil." Rulers ought to be a terror to terrorists. "Wilt thou, then, not be afraid of the power? do that which is good, and thou shalt have praise of the same: For he [the ruler] is the minister of God to thee for good. But if thou do that which is evil, be afraid; for he beareth not the sword in vain: for he is the minister of God, an avenger to execute wrath upon him that doeth evil."

What does the Bible have to say about war? How can a believer countenance war? Could he? Should he? Are we to be pacifists? No. But as individuals, we are to show love.

Number three: it is a time to repent. All the prayer in the world is not going to do any good unless we repent. Joshua was faced with an insignificant city named Ai in his conquest of Canaan. And Joshua was riding the coattails of victory until he came to little Ai.

The people didn't pray over Ai. As a matter of fact, there was sin in the camp. But they sallied forth to war against Ai with a handful of troops, and that little insignificant nation brought great devastation to the people of God. Joshua then got on his face before God and began to pray, "Oh, God, why did you allow this?" And God said, "Joshua, get up. Israel has sinned. Deal with the sin, Joshua."

What was God saying? That we cannot use prayer as a smokescreen to hide our sin. We can pray and pray and pray, but there must be something more: "If my people, which are called by my name, shall humble themselves, and pray, and seek my face, and turn from their wicked ways . . ." (2 Chronicles 7:14). Do you think we can ask God to bless our filth, our debauchery, our immorality, our mayhem against the unborn? No. We, as a nation, must repent. It's time to repent.

Number four: it's a time to speak. We need to speak out. We need to speak up. As the night grows darker, the saints need to grow brighter. All that happened was based on a philosophy, an idea that came out of the hearts of wicked and violent men. It first started in their heads. They had a concept, they had an idea, they had a distortion, and then they acted it out.

You cannot kill an idea with a bomb. You cannot shoot it down with a bullet. The only thing that will overcome an idea is a better idea. And that better idea is the Gospel of Jesus Christ. Would to God we had pulpits across America aflame with righteousness, opening the Word of God and saying, "Thus saith the Lord, thus saith the Lord . . ." Would to God in our neighborhoods we would share the love of Jesus, that we would live the truth, tell the truth, speak the truth, believe the truth, love the truth. Truth is greater than error. It's a time to speak.

Number five: *it's a time to unite.* I'm getting a little weary of hyphenated Americans, Americans with a prefix. I'm this kind of an American, I'm that kind of American. Let's just be Americans and love one another and respect one another and give one another the freedom to decide what to believe. We're not trying to coerce anybody; let's come together.

Isoroku Yamamoto, the admiral who led the Japanese in the attack at Pearl Harbor so long ago, said afterwards, "I had intended to deal a fatal blow to the American fleet by attacking Pearl Harbor. I fear that all we have done is to awaken a sleeping giant and fill him with a terrible resolve." And I believe these terrorists have done exactly the same thing. I believe they have awakened a sleeping giant. We'll never all be alike, look alike, act alike, or believe alike. But let's unite our hearts and stand together against this evil.

Last of all: it is a time to pray. Gather your family and pray. Gather your neighbors and pray. Go to your schools and pray. Go to your classes and pray. Let us pray and pray and pray that God's kingdom will come and that God's will will be done on earth as it is in heaven.

If you've never given your heart to Jesus Christ, if you've never trusted him as your personal Lord and Savior, you need to do so. The best thing you can do for yourself, for your family, for your city, for your nation, and for your world is give your heart to Jesus. Not to say, "my country, right or wrong," but to say, "Oh, God, I'm the one that's wrong. Be my God. I give you my heart, my soul, my life." I am not promising that you'll get an emotional feeling. You may or you may not. I don't mean that you'll sprout wings and get a halo. You'll have to grow as a Christian. But Christ *will* come into your heart. Your sins will be forgiven. Heaven will be your home. He'll never leave you or forsake you. The only reason you can be saved like this is because Jesus died for your sins on the cross and paid your sin-debt. You can receive the gift of salvation today and be saved.

EIGHT

TRUTH, TEARS, ANGER, AND GRACE

Timothy J. Keller

"Peace I leave with you; my peace I give you. I do not give
to you as the world gives. Do not let your hearts be troubled
and do not be afraid."

JOHN 14:27, NIV

Let me call you to worship today [Redeemer Presbyterian Church, New York City, September 16] in a quiet way, a way that's appropriate today, this week.

In 1 Thessalonians 4, Paul says to Christians, "Grieve, but don't grieve as those without hope." Paul is saying that there are two opposite mistakes you can make in the face of tragedy, death, and suffering. On the one hand, you can try to avoid grief. You can try to avoid weeping. You can try to put it out of your mind and get past it right away. That will either make you hard and inhuman or else it will erupt later on and devastate you.

The other mistake is to grieve without hope. The Bible indicates that the love and hope of God, and the love and hope that come from one another, have to be rubbed into our grief the way you rub salt into meat to keep it from spoiling. Your grief will make you bleaker and weaker or it will make you far more wise and good and tender, depending on what you rub into it. That is why we are here today [at Redeemer Presbyterian Church, New York City, September 16]. We are here not just to weep but to rub hope and love into our tears.

When John the Baptist was cut down in the middle of his

life in an unjust attack, that is what his disciples did in Matthew 14:12. First, they came, took up his body, and buried it. That is the grieving. But then they went and told Jesus.

All week [the week of September 11] we have been bearing up under an incredible load. Now it is time to tell Jesus. It is time to lay it at his feet. If you go and tell Jesus about your trouble and sorrows and all that is on your heart, he will speak to you. He will say something like, "That soul that on Jesus has leaned for repose I will not, I will not, desert to its foes. That soul though all hell should endeavor to shake, I'll never, no never, no never forsake."

Let us pray.

Almighty and most merciful God, you are the consolation of the sorrowful, you are the support of the weary. Look down now in tender love and pity on us whose joy has been turned into mourning, so that while we mourn and grieve, we may not have our hearts darkened, but rather might learn wisdom and grow strong in hope; that we might resign ourselves into your hands to be taught and comforted, remembering all your mercies and promises and love in Jesus Christ, who brings life out of death and can turn all grief into deep and eternal joy.

In our midst today we have people whose hearts are broken. Father, others can work on broken buildings and broken bodies, but only you can heal the broken souls, the fears, the grief, the rage, the despondency. Some of us have come very close to death, some of us have people dear to us who have died. Many of us are shattered. Bind us up.

Father, as your people, make us what we need to be for our city.

To a great degree, Father, we have been participating in the self-absorption of the great cities of our world. People come to the cities to take, to get, to build themselves up, to build up their resumés, to consume. Father, we ask that you get us out of ourselves. We ask that you humble us and purify us. Make us servants. Make us what we need to be in order to show the glory and love of Jesus to the people around us. Help us to be what the city needs us to be now, the kind of people the city needs us to be, the kind of neighbors and citizens we need to be.

Lastly, we pray for the churches of the city. Make us wise enough to know how to work together and use our resources to meet the needs. Make us generous. Teach us how to be Christian communities in a place that might be harder than ever to be a Christian community economically, socially, and physically. Father, we ask that you will protect us by your power and nurture us with newness and the sense of your presence. Fill us with your peace so we can be like Jesus, who came not to be served but to serve and give his life for many. We ask all this in Jesus' name, amen.

Our Scripture reading is the famous passage where Jesus is at the tomb of Lazarus in John 11:20-27, 32-35, 38-40, 43-46, 53.

> When Martha heard that Jesus was coming, she went out to meet him, but Mary stayed at home.

> "Lord," Martha said to Jesus, "if you had been here, my brother would not have died. But I know that even now God will give you whatever you ask."

Jesus said to her, "Your brother will rise again."

Martha answered, "I know he will rise again in the resurrection at the last day."

Jesus said to her, "I am the resurrection and the life. He who believes in me will live, even though he dies; and whoever lives and believes in me will never die. Do you believe this?"

"Yes, Lord," she told him, "I believe that you are the Christ, the Son of God, who was to come into the world."

. . . When Mary reached the place where Jesus was and saw him, she fell at his feet and said, "Lord, if you had been here, my brother would not have died."

When Jesus saw her weeping and the Jews who had come along with her also weeping, he was deeply moved in spirit and troubled. "Where have you laid him?" he asked.

"Come and see, Lord," they replied.

Jesus wept.

. . . Jesus, once more deeply moved, came to the tomb. It was a cave with a stone laid across the entrance. "Take away the stone," he said.

"But, Lord," said Martha, the sister of the dead man, "by

this time there is a bad odor, for he has been there four days."

Then Jesus said, "Did I not tell you that if you believed, you would see the glory of God?"

. . . When he had said this, Jesus called in a loud voice, "Lazarus, come out!" The dead man came out, his hands and feet wrapped with strips of linen, and a cloth around his face.

Jesus said to them, "Take off the grave clothes and let him go."

Therefore many of the Jews who had come to visit Mary, and had seen what Jesus did, put their faith in him. But some of them went to the Pharisees and told them what Jesus had done. . . . So from that day on they plotted to take his life.

This is God's Word.

Mary and Martha were facing the same problem we face today. They are looking at a tragedy and saying, "Where were you, Lord, in all of this? How do we make sense of this?" Jesus moves through the ruins with four things: truth, tears, anger, and finally grace. The truth he wields with Martha; the tears he sheds with Mary; the anger he directs at the tomb; and the grace he extends to everybody. Let's look at the way those four things fit together.

Let's begin with the tears of Jesus. What do we learn from

them? When Jesus reaches Mary, she asks him a major theological question. "Lord, why weren't you here? You could have stopped this." She asked him a question, but he couldn't even speak. He just wept. All he could do is ask, "Where have you laid him?" He is troubled. He is deeply moved.

This reaction is startling because when Jesus entered this situation, he came with two things that you and I don't have. First, he comes in knowing why it happened. He knows how he is going to turn it into a manifestation of the glory of God. He knows what he is going to do, and that in ten minutes they will all be rejoicing. When you and I enter into these tragic situations, we have no idea.

The second thing he had was power. He could do something about the problem. You and I can't do a thing to undo it. Yet still he weeps. Why? Why doesn't he just come in and say, "Wait until you see"? If you knew you were about to turn everything around, would you be drawn down into grief, entering into the trauma and pain of their hearts? Why would Jesus do that?

Because he is perfect. He is perfect love. He will not close his heart even for ten minutes. He will not refuse to enter in. He doesn't say, "There's not much point in entering into all this grief." He goes in.

We learn two things from that. The first is simple but needs to be said: There is nothing wrong with weeping at a time like this. Jesus Christ was the most mature person who ever lived, yet he is falling into grief. It is not a sign of immaturity or weakness. The people who are more like Jesus don't avoid grief.

They find themselves pulled into the grief of those who are hurting. There is something very right about that.

Jesus' tears also suggest something about our need to "fix it." There are a lot of people who are coming to New York to fix things. We are glad for them. They will try to fix the buildings. We need that. And eventually they will leave.

But when Jesus weeps, we see that he doesn't believe that the ministry of truth (telling people how they should believe and turn to God) or the ministry of fixing things is enough, does he? He also is a proponent of the ministry of tears. The ministry of truth and power without tears isn't Jesus. You have to have tears.

Do we do volunteer work? Yes. Do we help the people who have been displaced? Do we help the people who are bereaved? Yes. But consider this. Over the next months and years, New York may become a more difficult, dangerous place to live economically, politically, vocationally, or emotionally. It feels like it today, does it not? But if that happens, let's stay. Let's enter into the problems.

The city is going to need neighbors and friends and people who are willing to live here and be part of a great city. It may be more difficult and expensive just to be Redeemer Presbyterian Church for the next few months and years, I don't know. But if it is, the best thing we can do for the city is to stay here and be ourselves, even though it might cost more money or take more time. Maybe we are going to have to be a little less concerned about our own careers and more concerned about the community. So let's enter in. Let's not just "fix it."

Let's weep with those who weep. This is the first lesson about suffering, learned from the tears of Jesus.

The second thing we learn about suffering we learn from the anger of Jesus. Did you notice anything in the text I read that indicated that Jesus was angry? In verse 33, when Jesus saw Mary and the others weeping, it says, "He was deeply moved in spirit and troubled." But the original Greek word means "to quake with rage." In verse 38 as Jesus came to the tomb, it says he was "deeply moved." The original Greek word there means to roar or snort with anger like a lion or a bull. So the best translation would be, "Bellowing with anger, he came to the tomb." That must at least mean that his nostrils flared with fury. It might mean that he was actually yelling in anger.

This is relevant to us because we are all going through this corporately. Our shock and grief are giving way to fear and anger. There's a lot of rage around. In this passage, Jesus is filled with rage. So are we. What does Jesus do with it?

There are two things he does *not* do. First, he does not become a "Job's friend." Do you know what a "Job's friend" is?

In the book of Job, a series of terrible things happened to Job. His children died, he lost all of his money, and he became sick. Job's friends said, "Clearly, you are not living right! God must be judging you for your sins or these bad things would not happen."

Does Jesus speak that way to Mary and Martha? Is he angry at them or at the victims today? Does he say, "If this young man, Lazarus, is cut off in the prime of life, he must be receiving judgment for his sins"? No. He is not mad at them.

He is also not mad at himself. Isn't that interesting? Here is the one who claims to be God, who could have prevented this, now filled with rage, but not at himself. He says to Martha, "I am the resurrection and the life," one of the most stupendous claims anyone has ever made. He doesn't just say, "I am a healer." He says, "I am the resurrection and the life. I am the offer of life." He is claiming to be God! But when he gets to the tomb, he does not demonize anyone, including the victims, and including God.

I bring this up because everyone who is speaking publicly about this event must put it into a narrative structure to make sense of it. You cannot make sense of things unless you find a story line. There are two story lines that people are using today that Jesus is rejecting here.

The first story line is that this is happening because America is being judged for its sins. Interestingly enough, the left and the right are both using it. People on the left are saying that America asked for it because of our social injustice. People on the right are saying, "Look at all our immorality! God is punishing us." In both cases, the story line is "God is punishing us." Blame the victims.

Let's think biblically about this. How do you decide whether God is mad at you personally or at your nation? How do you know whether God is mad at you or pleased with you? Do you decide by looking at how life is going? No. Jesus Christ—who was a pretty good person, don't you think?— had a lousy life! Rejection! Loneliness! Everything went wrong!

In Luke 13 some people come up to Jesus and ask about

two incidents. One was a political massacre in which a group of people were killed by Pilate. In the other incident, a tower fell on thirteen people. The question was, were they being judged? Were they worse sinners than the others?

Do you know what Jesus says? *No.* And then he asks, "Why don't *you* repent?"—almost as if he is irritated with the question. How do I decide whether God is mad at me or pleased with me? I read the Bible. The Bible says, "Love God, love your neighbor." If I am not doing that, he is mad at me. If I am doing that, he is pleased with me. I can't decide, "I just lost my job, so he is mad at me." "I was just in a car accident. I am paralyzed. He must be mad at me." That's not how it works! Jesus did not suffer for us so that we would not suffer. He suffered so that *when* we suffer, it makes us like him. The story line that God is judging America for its sins is not a good one. Jesus is not mad at the victims.

There is another story line that seems to have more justification to it, and for that reason is somewhat dangerous.

This second story line is to demonize our enemy. *We* represent goodness. *They* are absolute evil. There is more warrant to this story line because what happened *was* evil. Justice has to be done. But that story line overreaches. Miroslav Volf is a Croatian Christian who has been through his share of suffering. It so happened that he was speaking at the United Nations prayer breakfast on September 11. He put it this way: "Enormous poison comes into my heart and into the culture of the world if I forget" that enormous problems happen "when I exclude my enemy from the community of humans and when I exclude myself from the community of sinners," when I forget that my enemy is not a subhuman monster but a human being, when I forget that I am *not* the perfect good but also a flawed person. But by remembering that, my hatred doesn't kill me or absorb me, and I can actually go out and work for justice.

Jesus does not conform to the second story line. He does not say, "I am mad at God. Demonize God. Demonize Middle Easterners. Demonize anybody who is Muslim. Shoot out their windows or their mosques." What does he do with his rage? He does not direct it against the people who have done this or against God. He focuses his rage on death itself. He is angry at the tomb. And this is the story line that the best leaders are using.

Jesus says, "I am going to turn this death into a resurrection. I am going to bring out of this something even greater than was there before."

That's the gospel story line, by the way. Out of the cross comes the resurrection. Out of the weakness comes real strength. Out of repentance and admitting you are weak comes real power. Out of giving away and serving others comes real strength. Out of generosity and giving your money away comes real wealth. That's the gospel story line.

Our most effective civic leaders are not saying we are being judged and they are not saying we are completely good and our enemies completely evil. What they are saying is that we can bring something even better out of this horrible event. Out of this death we can bring a resurrection!

Think about it. New York is filled with people who don't give a rip about New York. All they wanted to do was to get ahead. There was so much fun, so much money around.

Now do you want to be a part of it? Here is what could happen. What if New York became a community? Through this death couldn't there be a resurrection? Instead of a bunch of self-aggrandizing individuals and individualists, what if we actually became a community? What if the United States was truly humbled in realizing we are part of the rest of the world? We are not invulnerable. At the same time, we would become prouder in the best sense, in terms of the democracy project that we are. Out of this loss of goodness can come something even better. Out of this death we can see a resurrection. We can be a better city, better people, a wiser and better country. That is the right story line, and it actually incorporates what little truth there is in the others—our need to humble ourselves, to recognize the need for change and to do justice.

Here's the point. Unless you learn how to handle your anger, unless you know what story line to put it into, you can be railing and angry against America or railing and angry against God. Or railing against the demons out there who all look alike, so we can beat them up when we see them on the street.

Or out of this death can come a resurrection. That is what you should do with your anger. Don't get rid of it—be angry at death! "Rage against the dying of the light." Say, "I'm going to put this light on. I am going to make it brighter."

Somebody says, "That's pretty hard to do. First you tell

me to keep my heart open and weep with those who weep. Then you tell me not to use my rage in a way that short-circuits that whole process. I don't know if I can manage that!"

That is why Jesus gives us a third thing. It's the ministry of truth—not just his tears, not just his anger, but truth. He says to Martha, "I am the resurrection and the life. Do you believe this?"

The governor and mayor [of New York], whether they know it or not, are using the gospel story line. It's the best one there is. The moralistic story line is, "We are the good people. You are the bad people." That doesn't really help much in the long run. When your stance is, "We are the good people. We have been telling you that you have been sinning and now you finally got what you deserved," it doesn't work terribly well.

The gospel story line is the one that works. To the extent that it is working in our culture right now, we can bring a better city out of the ashes. But Jesus says, "I can give you something so much more. If you want an even greater resource—the ultimate power to handle this apart from a kind of altruistic wishful thinking—you have to believe."

He looks at Martha and says, "I can give you this power, but do you believe that I am the Son of God who has come into the world, that I am the one from heaven who has come down to this planet to die and rise again? Do you believe that?" He has a reason to ask, "Do you believe?" Because unless you believe that he is the Son of God who has come into the world, you don't have access to this incredible thing I am about to tell you. Martha says, "Yes, I do."

Do *you*? I hope you do. What I am about to tell you is contingent on your having a personal encounter in faith with the Son of God. Here is what he offers—not a consolation but a resurrection. What do I mean by that?

Jesus does not say, "If you trust in me, someday I will take you away from all this." He does not say, "Someday if you believe in me, I will take you to a wonderful paradise where your soul will be able to forget about all this." I don't want a place like that right now. I am upset and mad about what we have lost.

But Jesus Christ does not say he will give us consolation. He says he is giving us resurrection. What is resurrection? Resurrection means "I have come not to take you out of the earth to heaven but to bring the power of heaven down to earth—to make a new heaven and new earth and make everything new. I am going to restore everything that was lost, and it will be a million times better than you can imagine. The power of *my* future, the power of the new heaven and new earth, the joy and the wholeness and the health and the newness that will come, the tears that will be gone, and the suffering and death and disease that will be wiped out—the power of all that will incorporate and envelop everything. Everything is going to be made better. Everything is going to be made right."

Every year or so, I have a recurring nightmare that my wife is very flattered by. The nightmare is that my wife dies. Something has happened to her, and I'm trying to make it without her. My wife is very flattered by it because it is obviously my greatest fear.

But let me tell you something really weird. I almost like having the nightmare now. Do you know why? Because the first minute after I wake up is so unbelievably great! To wake up and say, "Oh my, it was only a bad dream. Everything bad I was living through has come untrue." It is not like being awakened to have someone give me something to make it better, in the sense of "Here's another wife." No. What I like about waking up is that the dream becomes untrue! It is a wonderful feeling to say, "It is morning. It was only a bad dream!"

Do you know what Jesus Christ is saying when he says, "I am the resurrection"? He is not saying that he will give us a nicer place. He is going to make everything that happened this week [the week of September 11] be a bad dream. He is not just giving you a consolation. He is going to make it come untrue. He is going to incorporate even the worst things that have ever happened to you. They will be taken up into the glory that is to come in such a way that they make the glory better and greater for having once been broken.

No one puts this truth better than Dostoevski. In *The Brothers Karamazov,* there is this fascinating passage: "I believe like a child that suffering will be healed and made up for, that all the humiliating absurdity of human contradictions will vanish like a pitiful mirage. In the world's finale, at the moment of eternal harmony, something so precious will come to pass that it will suffice. It will comfort all resentments. It will atone for all the crimes, for all the blood that has been shed, that it will make it not only possible to forgive but to justify everything that happens."

I feel like I am looking into a deep abyss when he says that. I know what he means. What he is trying to say is that we are not just going to get some kind of consolation that will make it possible to forget. Rather, everything bad is going to come untrue.

At the end of *Lord of the Rings,* the hobbit Sam, who thought everything was going wrong, wakes up and the sun is out. He sees Gandalf, the great wizard. To me, this is the quintessence of Jesus' promise. Sam says, "Gandalf, I thought you were dead. I thought I was dead. Is everything sad going to come untrue?" The answer of Jesus is, "Yes." Someday will be the great morning, *the* morning, not m-o-u-r-n-i-n-g but m-o-r-n-i-n-g, the great morning that won't just console us. Jesus will take all of those horrible memories, everything bad that has ever happened, and they will actually be brought back in and become untrue. They will only enrich the new world in which everything is put right—everything.

Do you believe this? Jesus says, "Do you believe this?" You say, "I want to believe this." If Jesus is the Son of God who has come from heaven, if he is the incarnate Son of God who died on the cross so that we could be forgiven, so God could someday destroy evil and suffering without destroying us, he paid the penalty so that we could participate in this.

Do you believe the Gospel? If you believe the Gospel, then you have to believe that. There are a lot of people in this room [at Redeemer Presbyterian Church] who do believe the Gospel, but they haven't really activated it this week. That is what I am here to help you do. You have not thought about that.

Your heart hasn't leapt. You haven't wept when you thought about it. I hope today is a start!

If, on the other hand, you do not really believe that Jesus is the Son of God, I ask you to keep coming and explore it. Jesus says, "Unless you believe in me, all that is just a pipe dream." If there is a God up there who has never become human, and you are down here hoping that someday you will be good enough for him to take you to heaven, it won't work. But if you believe in a God who is willing to come to die, to resurrect the whole world, a God who would come into our lives, that is the Gospel.

C. S. Lewis at one point says, "If we let him, he will make the feeblest and filthiest of us into dazzling, radiant, immortal creatures pulsating through with such energy and joy and wisdom and love as we cannot now imagine. He will make us into bright, stainless mirrors that reflect back to God perfectly, though, of course, on a smaller scale, his own boundless power and delight in goodness. That is what we are in for, nothing less."

Do you believe that? "Do you believe this, Martha?" Then you can face anything.

Everyone is wondering what kind of power New York is going to put back. I know that God is going to put something back. In the new heavens and new earth, everything we have here—even the best things we have here —will be just a dim echo of what we are going to have there.

Finally, somebody says, "How do I know this is going to happen? I would love to believe this, but how do I know?"

There is one more thing in this story you have to recognize. Jesus offered tears, truth, and anger, but did you notice the last line of the story, the last line of the text I read? It said, "From that day on they plotted to take his life."

Now that Jesus had raised Lazarus from the dead, his enemies said, "Now he's got to go. He is the most dangerous man there is. We've got to get rid of him now."

Don't you think Jesus knew that when he was raising Lazarus from the dead? Yes, he did. Jesus Christ knew and made a deliberate choice. He knew that the only way to interrupt Lazarus's funeral was to cause his own. The only way to bring Lazarus out of the grave was to bury himself. The only way he could get Lazarus out of death was for himself to be killed. He knew that.

Isn't that a picture of the Gospel? We have a God who is so committed to ending suffering and death that he was willing to come into the world and share in that suffering and death himself. There are an awful lot of people praying to a general God—"I am sure that God somehow is loving us." I *don't* know that. Or rather, I know that only because Christianity alone of all the religions tells us that God lost his Son in an unjust attack. Only Christianity tells us that God has suffered.

When somebody says to me, "I don't know that God cares about our suffering," I say, "Yes, he does." They say, "How do you know?" If I were in any other religion, I wouldn't know what to say. But the proof is that he was willing to suffer himself.

I don't know why he hasn't ended suffering and evil by now,

but the fact that he was willing to be involved and that he himself got involved is proof that he must have some good reason. He cares. He is not remote. He is not away from us.

Isn't it amazing that Jesus was so different with Martha and Mary? Martha and Mary, two sisters with the same situation, same circumstances, same brother. They even had the same question. Martha and Mary asked Jesus the same question word for word. But in Martha's case, Jesus' words were almost a rebuke as he laid truth on her. In Mary's case, Jesus just wept with her. Why? Because he is the perfect counselor. Not like me. I try, but I tend to be a "truther." I tend to say, "I have all this information. I don't want to waste your time, so let me try to fix things." I want to say, "You need to know this and this and this." Sometimes you just need somebody to weep with you, and I am not the guy. Then sometimes you go to a counselor, and all the counselor wants to do is weep, when you really need somebody to tell you the truth and bring you up short.

But Jesus is the perfect counselor. He will always give you what you need. If you need truth, if you need tears, he will give it to you the day you need it. He will give it to you in the dosage you need it. He will give it to you in the order you need it. He is the only perfect counselor there is. You need to go to him. You need to get his tears, you need to get his truth, you need to get his anger. You need all those things, but most of all you need to get his grace. That is what you need most, and that is what he came to give. That is what we are going to keep giving here [at Redeemer Presbyterian Church].

Let's pray.

Now, Father, we ask that you give us the possibility of growth and healing as a congregation, as a people, and as a city because we have seen that your Son is the resurrection and he died to prove it. With that hope we can face the future. Now we ask simply that you apply this teaching to our hearts in the various ways we need it applied so that we are able to be the neighbors and friends the city needs us to be. We pray this in Jesus' name. Amen.

About the Contributors

LISA BEAMER is the wife of Todd Beamer, one of the heroes of Flight #93. Since the tragic events of September 11, she has appeared on major television programs including *Larry King Live* and was present at President Bush's address to the nation days after the attack. The mother of two boys (David, three and Drew, one), she is also expecting a third child.

MAX LUCADO is the pastor of Oak Hills Church of Christ in San Antonio, Texas. He is one of Christianity's best-selling authors for both children and adults. His books include *He Chose the Nails*, *In the Grip of Grace*, *You Are Special*, *You Are Mine*, *Tell Me the Story*, and *Tell Me the Secrets*.

R. KENT HUGHES is senior pastor of College Church in Wheaton, Illinois. He has authored a number of books including *Disciplines of a Godly Man*, *Abba Father: The Lord's Pattern for Prayer*, and fourteen of the books in the acclaimed Preaching the Word series, for which he also serves as the series editor.

JONI EARECKSON TADA, paralyzed for more than thirty years, is the founder of Joni and Friends, an organization dedicated to accelerating Christian ministry in the disability community. She has authored more than twenty books, including *Heaven: Your Real Home*, *O Worship the King* (coauthor), *When God Weeps*, and for children: *Tell Me the Promises*, *Tell Me the Truth*, and *I'll Be with You Always*. Those desiring information about Joni and Friends can write to P O Box 3333, Agoura Hills, CA 91376 or call 818-707-5664 or visit their website www.joniandfriends.org.

JOHN PIPER is senior pastor of Bethlehem Baptist Church in Minneapolis. A noted author, his books include *Desiring God, Future Grace, A Hunger for God, God's Passion for His Glory, The Legacy of Sovereign Joy, The Hidden Smile of God*, and *Seeing and Savoring Jesus Christ*.

JOSEPH (SKIP) RYAN is senior minister of Park Cities Presbyterian Church in Dallas, Texas. After graduating from Westminster Theological Seminary in Philadelphia, he planted Trinity Presbyterian Church in Charlottesville, Virginia, where he served as senior pastor for seventeen years before beginning his pastorate in Texas. He was involved in the founding of Westminster's extension campus in Dallas.

JOSEPH M. STOWELL is president of Moody Bible Institute in Chicago. He has authored *Far from Home* and *Perilous Pursuits*.

RAY PRITCHARD is senior pastor of Calvary Memorial Church in Oak Park, Illinois, a suburb of Chicago. His many books include *What a Christian Believes, Keep Believing, The Road Best Traveled, Man of Honor*, and *An Anchor for the Soul*.

ADRIAN ROGERS is senior pastor of the 25,000-member Bellevue Baptist Church in Memphis. He is also the founder and president of Love Worth Finding Ministries, a nationally syndicated television and radio ministry. Books he has written include *The Power of His Presence, Believe in Miracles but Trust in Jesus, Ten Secrets for a Successful Family*, and *The Lord Is My Shepherd*.

TIMOTHY J. KELLER is senior pastor of Redeemer Presbyterian Church, located on Manhattan Island in New York City. While teaching Practical Theology at Westminster Theological Seminary in Philadelphia in 1988, he was asked to investigate the needs and possibilities for a new church in New York City. Redeemer Presbyterian, with Keller as pastor, was the result.